FRANCIS FRITH'S

YORKSHIRE

REVISITED

ROBERT E PREEDY

The author's schooldays were spent in Chesterfield, which was also Francis Frith's home town. Robert E Preedy has spent his working life in broadcasting with both the BBC and ITV. His various jobs have included cameraman, researcher, vision mixer and promotions producer. For 13 years he was a continuity announcer for commercial television in Leeds. He also presents a weekly radio show for regional BBC.With his keen interest in local studies, he has published fourteen books and written numerous articles on various aspects of Yorkshire history from Victorian times. He recently completed his second book tracing the development of roller coasters in the UK and this year wrote the story of Batley Variety Club, and a history of Radio 270, the 60's pop pirate station off Scarborough. His Frith's books include West Yorkshire, Ilkley, Selby, and the Villages of Yorkshire. Away from broadcasting and writing, his business interests have included running two cinemas. The first was in Pickering from 1984, and the second in Wetherby where he now lives.

YORKSHIRE
REVISITED

PHOTOGRAPHIC MEMORIES

ROBERT E PREEDY

First published in the United Kingdom in 2003 by
Frith Book Company Ltd

Hardback Edition 2003
ISBN 1-85937-459-x

Paperback Edition 2004
ISBN 1-85937-942-7

British Library Cataloguing in Publication Data

Francis Frith's Yorkshire Revisited - Photographic Memories
Robert E Preedy

Frith Book Company Ltd
Frith's Barn, Teffont,
Salisbury, Wiltshire SP3 5QP
Tel: +44 (0) 1722 716 376
Email: info@francisfrith.co.uk
www.francisfrith.co.uk

Printed and bound in Great Britain

Front Cover: **WHITBY,** *The Quay Side 1913* 66267
Frontispiece: **STAITHES,** *The Harbour c1885* 18215

*The colour-tinting is for illustrative purposes only, and is not intended
to be historically accurate*

AS WITH ANY HISTORICAL DATABASE THE FRITH ARCHIVE IS CONSTANTLY
BEING CORRECTED AND IMPROVED AND THE PUBLISHERS WOULD
WELCOME INFORMATION ON OMISSIONS OR INACCURACIES

CONTENTS

FRANCIS FRITH: VICTORIAN PIONEER   7

YORKSHIRE - AN INTRODUCTION   10

SWALEDALE   13

WENSLEYDALE   29

NORTH YORK MOORS   57

NIDDERDALE   60

RIBBLESDALE   66

THE WHARFE TOWARDS WEST YORKSHIRE   70

WEST YORKSHIRE   87

SOUTH YORKSHIRE   90

COASTAL YORKSHIRE   104

INDEX   115

Free Mounted Print Voucher   119

FRANCIS FRITH
VICTORIAN PIONEER

FRANCIS FRITH, founder of the world-famous photographic archive, was a complex and multi-talented man. A devout Quaker and a highly successful Victorian businessman, he was philosophical by nature and pioneering in outlook.

By 1855 he had already established a wholesale grocery business in Liverpool, and sold it for the astonishing sum of £200,000, which is the equivalent today of over £15,000,000. Now a multi-millionaire, he was able to indulge his passion for travel. As a child he had pored over travel books written by early explorers, and his fancy and imagination had been stirred by family holidays to the sublime mountain regions of Wales and Scotland. 'What a land of spirit-stirring and enriching scenes and places!' he had written. He was to return to these scenes of grandeur in later years to 'recapture the thousands of vivid and tender memories', but with a different purpose. Now in his thirties, and captivated by the new science of photography, Frith set out on a series of pioneering journeys up the Nile and to the Near East that occupied him from 1856 until 1860.

INTRIGUE AND EXPLORATION

These far-flung journeys were packed with intrigue and adventure. In his life story, written when he was sixty-three, Frith tells of being held captive by bandits, and of fighting 'an awful midnight battle to the very point of surrender with a deadly pack of hungry, wild dogs'. Wearing flowing Arab costume, Frith arrived at Akaba by camel sixty years before Lawrence of Arabia, where he encountered 'desert princes and rival sheikhs, blazing with jewel-hilted swords'.

He was the first photographer to venture beyond the sixth cataract of the Nile. Africa was still the mysterious 'Dark Continent', and Stanley and Livingstone's historic meeting was a decade into the future. The conditions for picture taking confound belief. He laboured for hours in his wicker dark-room in the sweltering heat of the desert, while the volatile chemicals fizzed dangerously in their trays. Back in London he exhibited his photographs and was 'rapturously cheered' by members of the Royal Society. His reputation as a photographer was made overnight.

VENTURE OF A LIFE-TIME

Characteristically, Frith quickly spotted the opportunity to create a new business as a specialist publisher of photographs. He lived in an era of immense and sometimes violent change.

For the poor in the early part of Victoria's reign work was exhausting and the hours long, and people had precious little free time to enjoy themselves. Most had no transport other than a cart or gig at their disposal, and rarely travelled far beyond the boundaries of their own town or village. However, by the 1870s the railways had threaded their way across the country, and Bank Holidays and half-day Saturdays had been made obligatory by Act of Parliament. All of a sudden the working man and his family were able to enjoy days out and see a little more of the world.

With typical business acumen, Francis Frith foresaw that these new tourists would enjoy having souvenirs to commemorate their days out. In 1860 he married Mary Ann Rosling and set out on a new career: his aim was to photograph every city, town and village in Britain. For the next thirty years he travelled the country by train and by pony and trap, producing fine photographs of seaside resorts and beauty spots that were keenly bought by millions of Victorians. These prints were painstakingly pasted into family albums and pored over during the dark nights of winter, rekindling precious memories of summer excursions.

THE RISE OF FRITH & CO

Frith's studio was soon supplying retail shops all over the country. To meet the demand he gath-ered about him a small team of photographers, and published the work of independent artist-photographers of the calibre of Roger Fenton and Francis Bedford. In order to gain some understanding of the scale of Frith's business one only has to look at the catalogue issued by Frith & Co in 1886: it runs to some 670 pages, listing not only many thousands of views of the British Isles but also many photographs of most European countries, and China, Japan, the USA and Canada - note the sample page shown here from the hand-written Frith & Co ledgers record-ing the pictures. By 1890 Frith had created the greatest specialist photographic publishing company in the world, with over 2,000 sales out-lets - more than the combined number that Boots and WH Smith have today! The picture on the next page shows the Frith & Co display board at Ingleton in the Yorkshire Dales. Beautifully constructed with mahogany frame and gilt inserts, it could display up to a dozen local scenes.

POSTCARD BONANZA

The ever-popular holiday postcard we know today took many years to develop. In 1870 the Post Office issued the first plain cards, with a pre-printed stamp on one face. In 1894 they allowed other publishers' cards to be sent through the mail with an attached adhesive half-penny stamp. Demand grew rapidly, and in 1895 a new size of postcard was permitted called the court card, but there was little room for illustra-tion. In 1899, a year after Frith's death, a new card measuring 5.5 x 3.5 inches became the standard format, but it was not until 1902 that the divided back came into being, so that the address and message could be on one face and a full-size illustration on the other. Frith & Co were in the vanguard of postcard development: Frith's sons Eustace and Cyril continued their father's monumental task, expanding the number of views offered to the public and recording more

5		Trinity College, View from the Grounds				+
6	•	St Catherine's College		+		
7	•	Senate House & Library		+		
8	•				+	
9	•	Gerrard Hostel Bridge		+	+	+ +
30	•	Geological Museum				
1	•	Addenbrookes Hospital			+	
2	•	St Mary's Church			+	
3	•	Fitzwilliam Museum, Pitt Press &c			+	
4	•				+	
5	Buxton, The Crescent					+
6	•	The Colonnade				+
7	•	Public Gardens				+
8	•					+
9	•					+
40	Haddon Hall, View from the Terrace					+
	Miller's Dale					+

and more places in Britain, as the coasts and countryside were opened up to mass travel.

Francis Frith had died in 1898 at his villa in Cannes, his great project still growing. The archive he created continued in business for another seventy years. By 1970 it contained over a third of a million pictures showing 7,000 British towns and villages.

FRANCIS FRITH'S LEGACY

Frith's legacy to us today is of immense significance and value, for the magnificent archive of evocative photographs he created provides a unique record of change in the cities, towns and villages throughout Britain over a century and more. Frith and his fellow studio photographers revisited locations many times down the years to update their views, compiling for us an enthralling and colourful pageant of British life and character.

We are fortunate that Frith was dedicated to recording the minutiae of everyday life. For it is this sheer wealth of visual data, the painstaking chronicle of changes in dress, transport, street layouts, buildings, housing, engineering and landscape that captivates us so much today. His remarkable images offer us a powerful link with the past and with the lives of our ancestors.

THE VALUE OF THE ARCHIVE TODAY

Computers have now made it possible for Frith's many thousands of images to be accessed almost instantly. Frith's images are increasingly used as visual resources, by social historians, by researchers into genealogy and ancestry, by architects and town planners, and by teachers involved in local history projects.

In addition, the archive offers every one of us an opportunity to examine the places where we and our families have lived and worked down the years. Highly successful in Frith's own era, the archive is now, a century and more on, entering a new phase of popularity. Historians consider the Francis Frith Collection to be of prime national importance. It is the only archive of its kind remaining in private ownership. Francis Frith's archive is now housed in an historic timber barn in the beautiful village of Teffont in Wiltshire. Its founder would not recognize the archive office as it is today. In place of the many thousands of dusty boxes containing glass plate negatives and an all-pervading odour of photographic chemicals, there are now ranks of computer screens. He would be amazed to watch his images travelling round the world at unimaginable speeds through internet lines.

The archive's future is both bright and exciting. Francis Frith, with his unshakeable belief in making photographs available to the greatest number of people, would undoubtedly approve of what is being done today with his lifetime's work. His photographs depicting our shared past are now bringing pleasure and enlightenment to millions around the world a century and more after his death.

YORKSHIRE
AN INTRODUCTION

IF THERE WAS ever any uncertainty about the variety of scenery in Yorkshire, the media images of the past thirty years have left no doubt of it. TV shows, like 'The Last of the Summer Wine', 'Emmerdale Farm', and 'All Creatures Great and Small', and films such as 'The Full Monty', 'Little Voice', and 'The Dresser', have all taken the county in all its glory around the world - and let us not forget that film from 1935, 'Turn of the Tide'. Within Yorkshire's 4 million acres are some of the most varied views imaginable. The Yorkshire dialect, too, is heard daily on national radio and television - no longer do broadcasters have to have a standard BBC accent. Sporting characters like Freddie Trueman and Dickie Bird, and the chat show host Michael Parkinson, have given us their Yorkshire straight talk. Each of the photographs in this book undoubtedly say 'This is Yorkshire'. Scores of books have been written about the county, but here we will find images of

WEST BURTON, *The Bridge and Falls 1893* 33146

many less well-known towns and villages, all portrayed by the Frith photographers over a period of about one hundred years, capturing a living landscape frozen in time.

Each of the old Ridings has its individual look. Our journey takes us into the past lives of monks in the monasteries, the sheep farmers high up in the Dales, the affluent gentry with their Victorian houses, the workers in the teeming new cities, and the coal miners working the rich seams of South Yorkshire.

The perception of the south is that it is a land of industrial dereliction, but in between the steel mills and coal mines we can find some quite delightful old manorial villages. Just out of Sheffield on the way into Derbyshire are some charming little places, and within the Barnsley and the Doncaster areas there are many quiet rural hamlets that have a history going back a thousand years. The low lands to the east of Doncaster were tamed two hundred years ago and transformed from marshy wastelands into fertile agricultural fields. However, a small village like Elsecar was changed forever once coal seams were discovered, and here the heritage of its past is now illustrated perfectly in the town museum. The wealth created for the landowners is also on show in their magnificent houses: Wentworth Woodhouse, near Elsecar, demonstrates the amazing gulf between the lives of those who own land and those who do not .

The middle part of Yorkshire, the West Riding, originally extended down to Sheffield, and was the powerhouse for the industrialisation of manufacturing. Bradford and Leeds grasped the opportunities to trade in wool. A ready supply of sheep in the upper dales, and an ingenuity for inventing looms and spinning machines, meant that the West Riding was at the forefront of a global trade in textiles. Much of the vast wealth created was then invested in the splendid civic buildings which abound in the area. If we look up and make note of the dates inscribed on the top of these buildings, we can see the timescale of the rise in prosperity that transformed the stinking slums into the vibrant towns and cities of today.

The Northern Dales are without exaggeration the shining diamond within the cluster. The wide open valleys that comprise the National Park have at the same time a rugged and a tender side. Victorian authors and artists came here over and over again to capture the inspiration that shines from the landscape. In times past, though, these same hills were the scene of a feverish rush to exploit the buried minerals beneath the turf. All along Swaledale and Wensleydale there is evidence of lead mines and smelt mills, and of the stone quarries that provided the Yorkshire stone so familiar in Frith's pictures. Hidden in the dales and valleys are castles and monasteries that were once the power base for warring neighbours. The sight of Castle Bolton in Wensleydale offers a real glimpse of the powerful at work and pleasure. Many of the old properties that were sold to pay death duties in the early 20th century have certainly been lost, but a surprising number have been preserved and lovingly renovated, either for offices or luxury apartments. Whatever the new use of these buildings, we should be glad that demolition was not an option.

The Dissolution of the Monasteries hit Yorkshire harder than many counties. Henry VIII perceived resistance and unrest here, where there were Catholic strongholds. His decision to force the closure of so many wonderful places of worship affected not only the monks, but also the wider community that was part of the commercial enterprise associated with the powerful institutions. Many monasteries were self-supporting, producing their own food and clothing as well as exploiting mineral deposits in the surrounding land. The monks at Jervaulx, for instance, were the first to make the world-renowned Wensleydale cheese. The wealth the monasteries created was an irritation to the king, and when he decided to dissolve them, he did so with a unexpected viciousness. The roofs were stripped of lead, land was given to the favoured gentry, and the fate of some dissenting abbots was death by hanging. Explosives were used to finish off the job of demolition. All around the county there are reminders of this past. Much of the stone was reused for houses and villages, and many peasants were able to purchase the freehold of their homes, so in some respects the Dissolution was a positive means of

changing the power base in England. But the Dissolution meant the destruction of a part of history that had stood for possibly 900 years.

On the dramatic coast of Yorkshire, where the cliffs face the turbulent German Sea, we find quaint villages and Victorian spas. Scarborough was the first town to see the commercial possibilities of a seaside holiday, although in the early days it attracted the gentry for health reasons, rather than pleasure seekers from the urban West Riding. The tiny fishing villages clinging to the side of steep and constantly eroded cliffs are still here to stop and savour. The view over the bay from Ravenscar to Robin Hood's Bay is said to have helped George III temporarily escape from his mental madness. It has the same effect today on stressed city people, who can slow down and appreciate again the joys of nature.

I hope you find much pleasure in the pages of this book. Following in the footsteps of the Frith photographers is always a fascinating experience.

PATELEY BRIDGE, *General View 1893* 32021x

SWALEDALE

KELD, *Butt House c1950* K66046

The tiny and isolated village of Keld stands high up in Swaledale (1100ft), surrounded by beautiful walking country; it is a favourite with lovers of the wild northern dales. All around are waterfalls like Kisdon Force and Stonesdale Beck Falls, and overlooking the village looms the brooding height of Rogan's Seat (2204ft). In the village stands the old Chapel, rebuilt in 1860, and the Public Hall and Reading Room of 1926.

KELD, *The Butter Tubs c1950* K66052

On the journey from Keld and Muker towards Hawes in Wensleydale we can see this awe-inspiring rock formation, which is created by water erosion. This is the best view, but care must be taken on this very narrow road. Even more awe-inspiring is to imagine the journey over this pass for a horse and carriage.

REETH, *The Green 1913* 65527

At the end of the 19th century, this was a boom town for lead mining. High on the valley side, old workings can still be seen. Once the price of lead fell after the discovery of cheaper lead from Spain, the population of Reeth halved. Fortunately for the village, this was also the time of the new tourist industry: Victorians came in search of peace and tranquillity away from the industrial West Riding. The green is still surrounded by five inns. Here on the right is the old Temperance Hall, next to the Literary Institute, now the National Park Centre. The front of the Congregational church is still a beacon for worshippers in this well-conserved part of upper Swaledale.

GUNNERSIDE, *General View 1923* 74372

Here we see Gunnerside Beck rushing into the Swale. Village life is captured in the streets of the village - the Literary Institute (1877) still stands, now the post office and village hall. The old smithy has been here since 1795 - it is still open, and now also houses a small museum. The King's Head Inn is a focal point, and the Wesleyan Methodist chapel (1866) still dominates the west side of the village.

SWALEDALE
Low Row 1924 75744

The Old Gang Mine, one of
the oldest workings, is a few
miles from here, and would
have brought the miners to
the warmth of the Punch
Bowl Inn, which was built in
1638. To the left is Holy
Trinity church, consecrated
in 1841. It has been lovingly
restored, first in 1886 and
more recently in 1975, and
exemplifies the simplicity of
religious life in the quietest
of the Dales. During the
building of the vicarage in
1846, human bones were
discovered, thought to be
those of soldiers from a
skirmish between the
Dalesmen and the Scots
during the battle with the
Young Pretender in 1745.

GRINTON
The Church and the Bridge 1923 74370

The church of St Andrew was built by the monks of Bridlington Priory over 900 years ago. The original font was rediscovered and replaced in the 19th century. Next to the church is the old manor house, with gardens running down to the river. Next to the bridge is a house dated 1762, and the Bridge Inn next door still offers hospitality to travellers through this delightful village.

MARRICK, *The Abbey 1913* 65514

Described as the quietest spot in the dale, this is where Benedictine nuns chose to build their priory in 1158. The Dissolution forced closure in 1539, and the chancel now lies in ruins. The nave was rebuilt in 1811. Since being made redundant, the church has now been converted to an outdoors adventure centre for young people.

DOWNHOLME, *The Bridge 1913* 65518

Downholme, where stone houses slope down to the Swale, lies 5 miles west of Richmond. In the village is a 13th-century Norman church. Nearby Walburn Hall - now a farmhouse - was built in Elizabethan times for the Scrope family, and was used in the Civil War as a garrison for King Charles.

HUDSWELL BANK, *General View 1913* 65517

From here we can see Richmond to the east and the sweep of Swaledale to the west. The painter Turner was very fond of this place. In the village is a 19th-century church, and these peaceful woods are now the property of the National Trust.

RAVENSWORTH
The Castle 1913 65498

Just north of Richmond are the remains of this old Norman castle. Inside the keep, the massive fireplaces needed to keep this rather desolate monument warm can still be seen. The castle is unusual in that it was built in the lower part of the village; it is now overlooked by the church at Kirby Hill. Almost a forgotten castle, there are no plaques commemorating its existence, and it is now in private hands, standing on a farm surrounded by cattle.

RAVENSWORTH
The Village 1913
65496

A wide green provides a focal point for this traditional Yorkshire village. In this picture we see, left, the old school, in use until 1967, now the village hall. The Methodist chapel (1822), next, is still used. On the horizon is the tower of the church at Kirby Hill (left). Also in the village is the Bay Horse Inn (1857).

GILLING WEST
The Village 1913 65482

We are looking east towards the bridge over the beck. The village is only two miles from Richmond, but it retains its rural charm. The White Swan Inn on the left is 300 years old; third house from the right is the old Gilling Club for working men. Twenty years ago it was used by the scouts, but now it is a private house. At the furthest end of the village is a fountain (1897) and the remains of the pinfold for stray sheep. The village still has a working blacksmith.

RICHMOND
The Castle and the Bridge 1893 32275

We are looking past John Carr's Green Bridge towards the magnificent castle - a true picture of medieval England. The castle was built from 1071 by Alan the Red as a defence station at the gateway to Swaledale. Although the castle has never experienced a siege, it has remained a military base, with barracks built inside the walls during the First World War to house conscientious objectors.

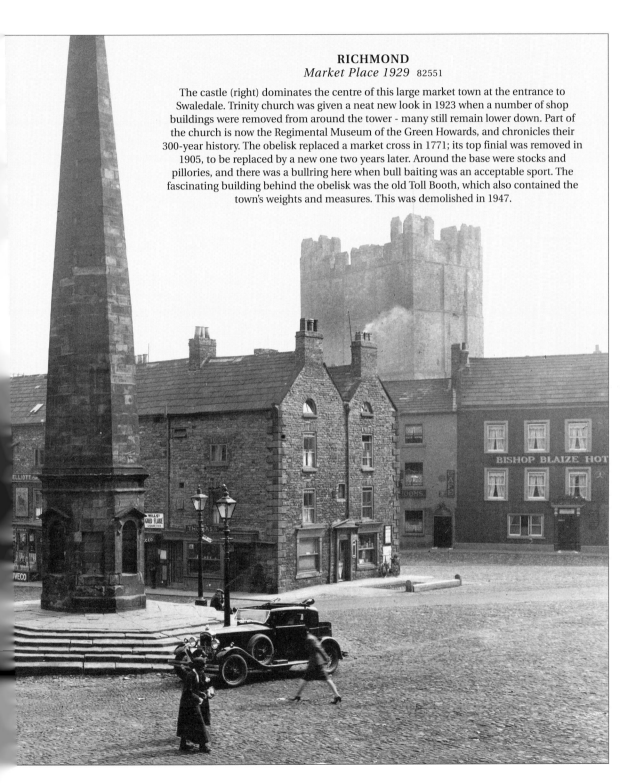

RICHMOND
Market Place 1929 82551

The castle (right) dominates the centre of this large market town at the entrance to Swaledale. Trinity church was given a neat new look in 1923 when a number of shop buildings were removed from around the tower - many still remain lower down. Part of the church is now the Regimental Museum of the Green Howards, and chronicles their 300-year history. The obelisk replaced a market cross in 1771; its top finial was removed in 1905, to be replaced by a new one two years later. Around the base were stocks and pillories, and there was a bullring here when bull baiting was an acceptable sport. The fascinating building behind the obelisk was the old Toll Booth, which also contained the town's weights and measures. This was demolished in 1947.

RICHMOND, *Millgate 1913* 65469

At the lower end of the market square, leading down to the Swale Falls, is Millgate - little changed today. Castle Wynd to the right still leads us through some fascinating alleyways, and of course the castle itself still looks over this side of town.

RICHMOND
Frenchgate 1913
65464

From 1877, once the barracks had been built in Gallowgate, the cobbles of Frenchgate would have echoed to the sound of marching soldiers. The barracks and headquarters of the Green Howards closed in the 1920s, and the buildings were then used as an approved school. This street, where we are looking towards the town from the east, still possesses this fine mixture of architectural styles.

SCORTON, *The Village 1912* 66040

The village lies next to Bolton on Swale five miles east of Richmond; it has the largest walled green in the whole of the country. Its grammar school was founded in 1720, and the Roman Catholic Chapel and Hospital of St John provides recuperation care for the infirm.

SKEEBY
The Village 1913
65491

Skeeby was once on the trade route from the Great North Road to Richmond, just two miles further west. Here, looking east we see the old Wesleyan chapel (1861) to the left, now a guesthouse. Lime Cottage, jutting out near the end of the street, is dated 1904. On the near right is Tenby Cottage, next to the old post office.

SKEEBY, *The Village 1913* 65490

Further down the main road through the village we see the stream, which is still here, and in the distance St Agatha's chapel of 1849. The house on the left is now demolished. Behind it is the old 17th-century manor house, now restored.

WENSLEYDALE

HAWES, *Gayle 1906* 56008

At one time Gayle overshadowed its neighbour, Hawes,
half a mile away. But then the turnpike road was built, and
Gayle lost its eminence. Village working life was
dominated by mining and the mill, now restored; it stands
next to the Wensleydale creamery, famous for its cheese.
This road leads to Bainbridge. We see (centre) Force Head
Farm (1711), and on the right the steps remain outside the
bonny baby's house, which is dated 1695.

BAINBRIDGE
The Village 1924
75706

Water flows through the village from Semerwater 2 miles away, via the country's shortest river, the Bain. Here, next to the Ure, are mill cottages. Around the charming green we can see the old school (centre), later a billiard hall, now restored as a private house. Behind are High Hall and the Temperance Hall (1910). The Quaker Meeting House came in 1836, and next is Summerfield House, formerly an inn. Finally, on the right is the Wesleyan chapel of 1836. The bridge over the Ure was widened by John Carr in 1785.

BAINBRIDGE
The Green 1929
82600

It is five years after photograph 75706 was taken, and the green is still attractive for the villagers. Here carefree youngsters play safely on the grass, oblivious to the events that unfolded by the old stocks near the white fence.

STALLING BUSK, *The Church 1911* 63459

At the end of the road from Countersett is Stalling Busk, looking out over Semerwater. The village is much higher up from the scene of this photograph, and includes the newer St Matthew's parish church. This isolated ruined church and burial ground was abandoned in the 1920s, but it still retains an otherworldly atmosphere.

ASKRIGG
Market Place 1906 56018

It is seventy years before filming took place in the village for the James Herriot TV series 'All Creatures Great and Small'. Next to the water pump was the old bullring, part of the huge market that took place here until the 1795 turnpike bypassed Askrigg on its way to Hawes. The market cross dates from 1851. Behind it we can see the Wesleyan chapel (1878) and the Village Hall of 1906. The Apothecary's House is hidden behind the Sykes Commercial Hotel (left), which later became a temperance establishment - it was recently converted into the village store. Out of picture on the right is St Oswald's church, 14th-century and the largest in the Dale, with its cast windows imported from Munich in the 1880s.

ASKRIGG
Little Askrigg 1911
63470

In the manor of Little Askrigg we find this road junction - if we go right, we reach Carperby (4 miles) and Leyburn (12 miles). Behind Woodburn House, left, was the village brewery. The confectionery shop and the chemist's (right) are now private cottages.

ASKRIGG, *Ellerkin 1914* 67244

Behind the village on the northern part of the Dale is this seemingly endless stretch of fields and craggy hilltops.

NAPPA
The Hall 1889 21664

This interesting house was built on the north bank of the Ure in 1459 for the Metcalfes, an influential Wensleydale family. Thomas Metcalfe was Privy Councillor to the Duchy of Lancaster. The house contains a minstrels' gallery and a private chapel. In 1637 an L-shaped addition was made to the south-east corner. The last Thomas Metcalfe was involved in the South Sea Bubble, and on his death the house passed out of the family. It is still inhabited, but not open to the public.

CARPERBY
*The Village and
the Cross 1914*
67217

Youngsters enjoy the
sunshine and calm
just before the
outbreak of war in this
quiet village 8 miles
from Leyburn. Little
has changed over the
years. The square
house, centre, dates
from 1908.

CARPERBY
*The Village and
the Cross 1909*
61762

Further into the centre
we see the public
buildings of the village.
From the left are the
Wesleyan chapel
(1890), the old school,
now empty, and the
Friends' Meeting
House and burial
ground, dating from
1864. The market cross
bears the date 1674.

REDMIRE
The Village 1929 82588

Redmire lies 3 miles west of Leyburn. Lead mining was a major employer here, but now the stone quarrying is further north, leaving Redmire in peaceful seclusion. The Wensleydale Railway reached here in 1877 and lasted until 1954 - although a service was reintroduced in the tough winter of 1963. Happily the line, from Leeming to Leyburn, reopened in July 2003, with plans to extend to Hawes and Garsdale Head in future years. Today the already existing line to Redmire carries the occasional army tank from Catterick for manoeuvres on the moors. The stone pillar we see here was erected in 1887, and the village was supplied with lamps to commemorate the 50th year of Queen Victoria's reign. An electric lamp was fitted to the top of the pillar in 1977 to mark the 25-year reign of Elizabeth II.

REDMIRE
The Village 1909
61742

This road leads out of the village towards Carperby. Here we see North's House (centre), and Polly Miller's (left) - both named after fondly remembered former residents.

PRESTON-UNDER-SCAR, *General View 1911* 63448

The village hugs the huge limestone hillside, once the site of much lead mining and smelt mills. The addition of 'under-Scar' came in the 16th century to distinguish the village from other Prestons. In the village are the parish church (1862) and the Wesleyan chapel (1805). The path across the field would be a short cut from the railway line that ran just out of picture.

AYSGARTH
The Village 1908 60791

When the railway arrived in the village, life changed overnight. Victorian visitors came to look at old rural England - so different to their world in the overcrowded working cities of the West Riding. They came to see the spectacular falls, which powered the massive mill in the valley. Afterwards they could stay at the Yoredale Guest House (right) and buy provisions in Watson's Grocery next door - now specialising in Wensleydale cheese. At the end of the row, Cherry Tree Farm House still stands.

WEST BURTON, *The Village 1909* 61759

Without through traffic, this thousand-year-old village retains its rural traditions and sense of history. A century ago, West Burton was a lively farming village with a market and many shops. The villagers bought the green from the lord of the manor in 1969. The Black Bull dates from the early 18th century; it was a pub until 1924, and is now a house. The Methodist chapel behind dates from 1898, and the village hall was originally the Congregational chapel (1874).

WEST BURTON
The Bridge and the Falls 1893 33146

As Walden Beck cascades towards the Ure, it crosses under the Blue Bridge; it used to power the old mill downstream. We can still walk up to the Cauldron Falls and on to Hudson Quarry. From 1913 the mill provided the village with electricity, until the National Grid took over in 1948.

WEST WITTON
The Village 1911
63452

On their way to Aysgarth, carriages would pass through West Witton. The 17th-century coaching inn, right, was converted to a pub as late as 1983, and is now a guest house, complete with stables and mounting block at the rear. Further along the road is the Wesleyan Sunday School (1844) and the Methodist church of 1842. On the left is the old Fox and Hounds Inn, next to the medieval Catheral Hall.

WEST WITTON
The Heifer Inn
1911 63453

This 17th-century coaching inn is still open for travellers. Opposite was the old library and reading room, which was later used as additional accommodation for the Heifer Inn. A few years ago the horse trainer Ferdy Murphy bought this annexe for use by his visiting jockeys.

WEST WITTON
The Village 1911
63457

The stream ran down from Pen Hill through this pond to provide motive power for the corn mill over the road and below the Heifer Inn. When the mill was demolished the pond was filled in and grassed over for use as the village green - a generous act by two local benefactors. On the left is the old wool store and barn.

BELLERBY, *The Village 1929* 82575

Just north of Leyburn is this fine village complete with a large green. Here on the north side the duck pond is still here, looking very tranquil, but the village is prone to flooding, as the stream can easily burst its banks.

BELLERBY
The Village 1896
38266

From the 13th century, the village was part of the huge 3000-acre manor estate of the de Bellerbys. Rievaulx Abbey also farmed some 43 acres of land near the village. The tree is still here, and so is the Old Hall (left), dating from the 17th century. The church of St John (1874) can be glimpsed through the tree.

WENSLEY, *The Green 1906* 56003

This was such a tranquil place in 1906; but now it lies on the main Dales road from Hawes to Leyburn. The village was at the private entrance to Bolton Castle, and would have provided this massive stronghold with goods and trades. The castle dominates the northern side of the Dale; it was here that Mary Queen of Scots was imprisoned in 1568 and 1569 before her eventual execution in 1587.

WENSLEY, *From the Church Tower 1893* 33134

Once a busy market until the plague forced customers away, the village was then eclipsed by Leyburn. Holy Trinity church contains a Saxon cross, found in the 19th century, and the Bolton family pews, which came from the theatre in London's Drury Lane. It is said that the Duke fell in love with a singer in 'The Beggar's Opera' and kept her as his mistress for many years.

LEYBURN
Market Place 1934 86155

A busy market day in the huge square. Leyburn took over from nearby Wensley, after the plague ruined trade there. Now Leyburn is a magnet for tourists - we come to enjoy its old world charms. From the left, we see the great coaching inns, the Golden Lion and the Black Swan. In the centre is the Methodist church (1884), and in the distance St Matthew's church. The garage and its roof tea-garden, centre right, were converted to the tourist information centre and retail shops some four years ago.

LEYBURN
*The War Memorial
1923* 74377

Just in front of the
Town Hall (1856) is the
war memorial
remembering the ten
men who died in the
First World War, and
the ten who perished
in the Second. Near to
the site of this
memorial was the old
market cross, removed
in 1837.

HAUXWELL
*The Rectory, Birthplace of Sister
Dora 1913* 66039

Built in the late 18th century, this was
home to the Pattison family in the years
1825 to 1865. Dorothy Wyndlow Pattison
was born on 16 January 1832, the
eleventh child and tenth daughter of the
rector of Hauxwell. After her schooling
she wanted to join Florence Nightingale
in the Crimea, but her father forbade
this. Instead she became a pioneer of
civil nursing, spending much of her life
in Walsall, where she ran the Cottage
Hospital. Her skills were such that she
carried out much work normally done by
surgeons. She died on Christmas Eve
1878 in Walsall, where a statue
commemorates her life. The Rectory, her
birthplace, was demolished in 1958.

HAUXWELL
The Village 1913 66037

Children from Yew Tree Farm pose outside their gate for the photographer - a major event in this quiet village, well off the main Leyburn road. The only change to this scene is that the house on the left is now a barn, which is unusual.

MIDDLEHAM
The Castle and the Cross
c1950 M70069

These impressive ruins were once the home and meeting place for the most powerful men in the land. As Richard Neville, Earl of Warwick looked out over his land, he would have seen acres of the Yorkshire countryside full of villages (little changed today). After Neville was killed in battle, another Richard, the Duke of Gloucester, lived here before becoming King Richard III. In this part of lower Wensleydale it is a curious feeling to walk in the shadow of so much power.

MIDDLEHAM, *The Manor House 1914* 67200A

Monks from nearby Jervaulx Abbey began the tradition of horse breeding in this dale. Behind the Georgian Manor House are the stables used by three generations of the famed horse trainers, the Peacock family. The streets of the village still echo to the sounds of racing horses on their way to the moors for training and a good hearty run.

COVERHAM
The Abbey Church 1926
79044

In between the dramatic hills of Great and Little Whernside, Coverham lies in a hollow 2 miles west of Middleham. It was a peaceful place for the establishment of an abbey, which endured from 1202 to 1536. The ruins are now part of a private house. Also in the village near the waterfall is Holy Trinity church, restored in 1878. A 17th-century manor house completes the idyllic picture.

JERVAULX ABBEY, *The Chapter House 1896* 38276

Lying peacefully on the banks of the Ure, the land was given to the monks by Conan, son of Alan the Red, who built Richmond Castle. The abbey was established in 1156, and it gained its revenue from sheep breeding and mining for coal and iron. The monks were the first to produce Wensleydale cheese, using sheep's milk. Jervaulx was destroyed in 1537 by Henry VIII - the last abbot was hanged at Tyburn, and the king took his revenge by blowing up the building with gunpowder.

EAST WITTON
The Village 1918 68200

To the west of Jervaulx lies this pretty village, nestling around the spacious green. The centre is overlooked by the 1100ft-high Witton Fell, and on the green is a huge boulder brought down by 20 horses in 1859. In the Farmery Mine a disaster in 1820 killed 20 men - their graves are in the churchyard. Another disaster had hit the village in 1796 when a fire destroyed much of the fabric, and it mostly had to be rebuilt. The Blue Lion Inn was in the hands of the same family from 1856 until 1989.

SPENNITHORNE, *The Church 1914* 67228

Spennithorne is situated just to the south-east of Leyburn. Part of the church was built from stone taken from Jervaulx Abbey after the Dissolution. The tower dates from the 14th century, and the chancel from the 17th. In the graveyard is a Russian cross taken from Sebastopol by Sir C Van Straubenzee.

SNAPE
The Castle 1896
38287

The castle was once the home of the powerful Neville family; now parts of their castle lie in ruins, although one side remains habitable. Catherine Parr, born here, became the Queen of England as the sixth wife of Henry VIII. Her fate was a lucky one: she became his widow and eventually remarried.

SNAPE, *The Village 1900* 45619

This delightful village, 2 miles south of Bedale, was once the support for the castle. Today visitors could easily miss Snape on their way to the popular arboretum with its unique collection of trees and shrubs from around the world at nearby Thorpe Perrow. The arboretum was created during the lifetime of Colonel Sir Leonard Ropner (1895-1977). His son Sir John carries on the tradition, and the stunning 85 acres of woodland attract an increasing number of visitors each year.

SCRUTON, *Scruton Hall 1900* 45615

The village, 3 miles east of Bedale, grew up around Scruton Hall, and contains a church, a rectory and a manor house. Scruton Hall was built in the Queen Anne style; it was demolished in 1956.

MASHAM
Market Place 1908 60696

A real sense of space is offered here in the market place. Masham market was granted trading rights from 1393. At one time 40,000 sheep could be traded in one day. Richmond complained about the competition, because Masham's market was always free of tolls. The coaching inn the King's Head (right) was also the tax and licence office until 1850. The church of St Mary dates from the 12th century, and outside is an even earlier carved Saxon cross. Also in the market place is the old grammar school, now holding primary classes. A stray German bomb fell here in 1941 after a raid on Teesside, and completely destroyed the White Bear Inn.

CRAKEHALL
The Village 1900
45605

Crakehall, 1 mile north of Bedale, is two villages in one - this is Little Crakehall, with its race (left) for three corn and flax mills. Just downstream is the restored water mill, now producing stoneground wholemeal flour. Here on the right is the former Primitive Methodist chapel of 1897, now a house. The barn is still here, but the central houses have been redeveloped. Great Crakehall to the right and up the hill has the village green with St Gregory's church, the school and the cricket ground.

STUDLEY ROYAL
The Park, the Temple of Piety c1885 18377

After the dissolution of Fountains Abbey, the land was eventually purchased by John Aislaby. He landscaped the fields and created the two lakes and the formal water gardens. Next to the round lake he built the Temple of Hercules in 1742, the year of his death. This temple, one of a number of temples and follies around the estate, was then redesigned as the Temple of Piety in 1781. Inside are busts of the Roman emperors Vespasian and Nero.

STUDLEY ROYAL
Fountains Hall c1885
18382

Fountains Hall in the Fountains estate was begun in 1742, and completed twenty years later. All the stone used in the building came from the ruins of the abbey, a hundred yards away. The Hall was lived in until the late 1950s. It was then acquired by the National Trust, who use it for an exhibition centre on this World Heritage Site.

RIPON, *The Cathedral from the South-East 1901* 47177

Stonemasons and glaziers from France and Italy built St Wilfred's first stone church on this site in 672. Reconstruction began in 1069, followed by the building we see today from 1180. The west front was added in 1220. The minster finally became a cathedral in 1836. Hidden in the crypt are the remains of the original St Wilfred's church. Lewis Carroll, the son of the first canon of the cathedral, visited his father here in Ripon over a span of twenty years. He was inspired by cathedral carvings of a lion, an elephant on the back of a turtle and the curious creatures carved on the misericords in the choir. He first told the tale of Alice in Wonderland in July 1862, after ten years of visits to Ripon and its magnificent cathedral.

RIPON
The Spa Baths 1914 67316

On the west side of the city, towards Fountains Abbey, stands the Spa Baths and Pump Room, opened on 24 October 1905 by Prince Henry of Battenburg. At that time you could avail yourself of an immersion spa bath and afterwards sip the sulphur water. Behind the foundation stone is a sealed box containing documents, coins and newspapers. Public swimming baths were added in 1936 - before this, changing rooms had been built alongside the river. The Spa Hydro opened in 1909, and the statue of the Marquis of Ripon was unveiled in the nearby park in 1912. A canal to the town was finished in 1773, and the railway arrived in 1848 - it survived until 1967. Ripon Racecourse opened in June 1900.

SKELTON ON URE, *Newby Hall c1965* S135004

Newby Hall was built by Sir Christopher Wren for the MP of Ripon, Sir Edward Blackett, during the 1690s. A hundred years later Robert Adam was commissioned to alter and redecorate the house as we see today. The statue of the horseman has an intriguing history. Originally it was modelled on the King of Poland, but when the bill for it was not paid, Sir Thomas Vyner brought it to England in 1675. It was then re-carved as a portrait of Charles II, and was erected in London before going to Lincolnshire in 1779. It has been here at Newby Hall since 1883.

BOROUGHBRIDGE
High Street 1907 58628

The Norman plan for settlements made Boroughbridge the 44th of the 400 new towns. The Romans had been here from AD 72, when they settled nearby at Aldborough about a mile away. In more modern times the town was a major coaching post on the great North Road, and many fine inns survive here. The first mail coach from London reached here on 16 October 1789 -superseded a century later by the railway. Just beyond the old Swan Hotel, centre left, is the entrance to Boroughbridge Hall.

BOROUGHBRIDGE
The Devil's Arrows 1895 35295

The three remaining millstone grit pillars (there were originally four)
have been here since the Bronze Age. They lie in a north-south axis
on the western edge of the town; they measure as high as 22ft 6in,
and are as big as the stones at Stonehenge. Each weighs about thirty
tons - they possibly came from the quarries at Knaresborough. The
fourth pillar was cut up and used as foundations for Penny Bridge
over the River Tut, which runs through the town.

NORTH YORK MOORS

RIEVAULX ABBEY *c1867* 3867

Lying in the tranquil Rye valley two miles west of Hemsley, this is the first Cistercian monastery in the North of England. It was built in 1131 by French monks; as well as leading their spiritual life, they were also shrewd businessmen. They managed huge sheep flocks for the wool trade, as well as iron smelting, glass production and leather tanning. After the Dissolution in 1538, the land and the buildings were given to the Duncombe Estate in Hemsley. Much of the village was built from the stone of the old abbey.

EASBY
Easby House 1913
65503

Here in the far north of the county, 2 miles south of Great Ayton, stands this 'Gentleman's Residence', built in Georgian times for the Emerson family. The estate included a private chapel, but this was closed in 1986. The house itself ceased to be inhabited in 1934, but in recent years it has been renovated back to its former glory.

THORNTON DALE, *Beck Isle Cottage c1965* T139062

Thornton Dale lies 2 miles east of Pickering. This much-photographed cottage stands alongside the beck, in which trout can still be seen. In the village are Lady Lumley's Almshouses. In 1656 she also gave a bequest for a hospital and a grammar school to be built in the village. Trade here came from corn milling, spinning and weaving, and paper manufacture. Beck Isle Cottage was once the home of the village laundry maid.

EGTON
The Bridge c1885 18181

This is seemingly a quiet place on the Esk Valley that runs down to Whitby, but this bridge was swept away in a flood on 23 July 1930. It was rebuilt in 1992 in the style of the original. The coming of the railway to Grosmont in 1845 did much to allow town dwellers a glimpse of a forgotten way of life. The Esk Valley line still runs along the route of the river through some beautiful scenery, with stops all the way. Visit Egton in August to enjoy the annual gooseberry show.

SLEIGHTS, *The Railway Crossing and the Footbridge c1960* S809007

The Esk Valley Railway from Whitby to the north-east was begun in 1835 and was completed in 1861. It was extended to join the Pickering to Grosmont line four years later.

NIDDERDALE

PATELEY BRIDGE, *General View 1893* 32021X

This charming village lies within the deep Nidd valley. Here looking down the High Street we see splendid views of Upper Nidderdale. A light railway came from Harrogate in 1862, and was much used during the construction of the reservoirs for Bradford Corporation. On the horizon are the remains of the many lead mines around Greenhow, which provided material for the roof of Fountains Abbey. Two miles out of Pateley are the 1100yd-long Stump Cross caverns, discovered in 1860 by miners.

HARROGATE
The War Memorial and Prospect Place 1923 74568

This is the view visitors would see from the main Leeds to Ripon road. The gardens for the Prospect Hotel (rebuilt in 1870) on the corner used to extend down to the road and over the site of the memorial. We can see two church towers on the horizon: to the left is the 1860 West Park United Reformed church, and behind the trees, looking out over the site of Harrogate's first railway station, is Trinity Church. The majestic war memorial dates from 1923.

HARROGATE, *Valley Gardens and the Tea House 1911* 63516

Visitors relax in the splendour of Valley Gardens, and tea is served from the Sun Pavilion. The spa trade declined in the 1920s - although more visitors came, they spent less money. The fashion for health spas was on the wane. But before the Great War, times were still genteel, and enjoyment came from simple pleasures.

HARROGATE
The Royal Pump Room
1902 48974

The discovery of spa water in 1571 led to a remarkable period in the town's history. Here in Low Harrogate hotels and stylish crescents were built, attracting a very high-class visitor. The Pump Room here was constructed in 1842 over the sulphur wells. Now it is a fascinating museum, where visitors are encouraged to sample the health-giving water. To the left is Hales Bar, a coaching inn from 1849, and behind the Pump Room is the Crown Hotel, rebuilt in 1847.

HARROGATE
The Kursaal 1911 63527

This £40,000 concert and dancing hall opened in 1903; the plans were by R J Beale and the noted theatre designer Frank Matcham. The old box office is still here, and displays the original ticket prices. The hall now seats 1,000, and is undergoing much-needed remedial work on the corroded concrete. The tree on the right was the second oldest in the town - it was removed after recent gale damage. The oldest tree survives at the Queen Parade end of Victoria Avenue.

KNARESBOROUGH, *The Viaduct and the River 1921* 71673

Here we have a world-famous scene: the peaceful Nidd dominated by the 338ft-long railway viaduct. The original viaduct of 1847 collapsed after heavy rain, and was rebuilt three years later. Overlooking this view are the remains of Knaresborough Castle, destroyed by orders of Parliament in 1644. Houses at the top of this picture date from 1721.

KNARESBOROUGH, *The River Nidd, the Rapids 1914* 67267

Punting on the river in pre-war days. Near here is Conyngham Hall, now a conference centre, but once the home of the toffee maker from Halifax, Lord Macintosh. The hall was built in 1796 on the site of Coghill Hall, a Tudor house from 1555. Another famous resident of Knaresborough, Jack Metcalfe, was born within sight of the castle in 1717. He was blinded by smallpox at the age of 6, but despite this setback led a full and active life. In 1765 he began his career as a master road builder, completing the construction of 200 miles across the North. His accurate measuring device, the Viameter Wheel, can be seen in the Castle Museum. Blind Jack Metcalfe died in 1810, aged 93, and is buried at Spofforth

RIBBLESDALE

INGLETON, *Thornton Foss 1929* 82733

The village nestles at the foot of Ingleborough, one of the famous Three Peaks, but it was the waterfalls walk that brought town dwellers to the area. Once the Settle to Carlisle railway had opened, which ran to the east of Ingleton, Victorian entrepreneurs laid out the 4-mile walk along the banks of the River Twiss towards Pecca Falls, Hollybush Spout and to this spot, where the forty foot cascade of Thornton Force surges into a natural amphitheatre. The return walk takes us along the River Doe with its dramatic gorge and water plunges.

SETTLE, *Castleberch Wells and Steps 1924* 75792

In this town we will find a fascinating mixture of alleyways, courtyards and shambles. Many of the houses date from the 17th century, after the Civil War; trade in the town increased dramatically once the Keighley to Kendal turnpike road opened, making Settle a premier coaching route. Two railways touched the town: the North West line was followed by the famous Settle-Carlisle line in 1876. Allow twenty minutes to climb these steps up to the summit of Castleberch, a limestone crag from where magnificent views look over to Giggleswick and beyond to Upper Ribblesdale.

LANGCLIFFE
General View 1921 71343

Langcliffe lies 1 mile to the north of Settle on the route towards the
majestic Three Peaks. Industry in the village included candle making
and paper production. The mill chimney is prominent in this
picture, together with the school, the Victorian church and the
Wesleyan chapel.

MALHAM COVE *c1881*
13666

Once water cascaded over this 240ft-high limestone cliff, but now it runs underground from the Tarn before it reaches this point. The spectacular falls last flowed across the 300-yard crag at the end of the Ice Age. At the top is the isolated Tarn House, now an outdoor centre, but once the Victorian meeting place for gentlemen of stature. Charles Kingsley stayed here, and found inspiration for his novel 'The Water Babies'. A century later the film was partly made at Denton Park, near Ilkley.

KETTLEWELL, *General View 1926* 79071

We are looking from Cam End over to Moor End. Cam Beck once powered the 13th-century mill. Next to the stream is the old Methodist chapel of 1860, now a house, but with gravestones still in the back garden. St Mary's church can be glimpsed in the middle distance. Many buildings in the village date from the 17th century, including Damside House (1681) and the Old Vicarage (1647).

THE WHARFE TOWARDS WEST YORKSHIRE

HUBBERHOLME, *The George Inn c1960* H130011

In this inn, formerly the vicarage, the centuries-old Hubberholme parliament met each year to auction the letting of 16 acres of rough upland pasture behind here. The proceeds were used to help the old people of the parish. On the other side of the Wharfe is the 12th-century church of St Michael and All Angels, given to the monks of Coverham Abbey in 1241. A memorial plaque in the graveyard marks the burial place of the ashes of J B Priestley (1894-1984), who loved and was inspired by this part of Upper Wharfedale.

STARBOTTON
From Moor End 1926
79081

Not far from the imposing Buckden Pike, here is a picture of tranquillity in the upper section of Wharfedale. The 17th-century cottages used to house lead miners, and there is evidence of an old smelt mill. The village has a Quaker burial ground and a former Methodist chapel. In the flood of 1686, there was a national appeal for help and assistance.

GRASSINGTON, *The Square 1926* 79060

A village has existed here for over 900 years. Celts and Vikings have settled here - many Danish and Norse words are still used by farmers. Church House (down to the left) dates from 1694, but Grassington's boom time was in the 18th century, when a Klondike rush of workers from Derbyshire and Cornwall came to work the lead mines - and the number of inns rose to five. Once the Dales Railway reached here in 1902, tourism took over as visitors came to soak up the charms of this attractive settlement.

ADDINGHAM
Farfield Hall c1955 A118006

The house was designed in the mid 18th century by Richard, Earl of Burlington. Later it was the home of the Bradford industrialist Samuel Cunliffe Lister, later Lord Masham. His statue has been in Manningham Park, Bradford since 1875. In recent years the house has been used as an old peoples' home by Bradford Council.

ILKLEY
Denton Park from the Cow and Calf Rocks 1914 67330

Through the famous Cow and Calf Rocks high up on Ilkley Moor, we can see the estate of Denton Park, once the home of the Fairfax family. After a fire in 1734 it was rebuilt by John Carr in fine Georgian style. The stone came from a quarry on the estate's land. The house was divided into three parts in 1919, and is now used as offices by a major building company.

ADEL
The Church 1891 28270

The Norman church of St John the Baptist stands in the north of
Leeds. It was built around 1150 on the site of a Saxon church, and
the south porch was added a decade later. Ancient animal symbols
festoon the porch - they represent the four evangelists. The inner
arch contains 40 beak heads, possibly suggesting the 40 days and
nights of Christ's wilderness fast. The ornate tomb on the left is
inscribed 'Until the day break and the shadows flee away'; it is a
monument to the Hirst family, and was first used in 1884.

BRADFORD
The Wool Exchange 1897 39512

The foundation stone for this £40,000 building was laid by Lord Palmerston in 1864.
This proud Gothic trade house was home to three thousand dealers, who traded wool from
West Yorkshire, the colonies and the Far East. It contains a number of statues of prominent
men of Bradford, which became a city in the year of this photograph. The Wool Exchange is
now sympathetically restored to a well-stocked book shop.

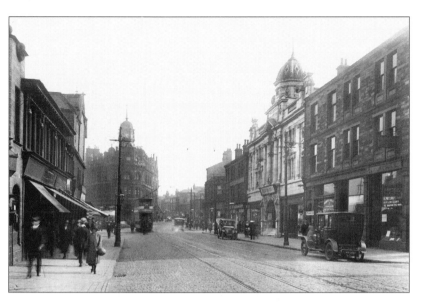

BRADFORD
Manningham Lane 1921
71623

We are travelling out of the city towards Manningham Park and on to Shipley and Bingley. This used to be a centre for entertainment, with the old Theatre Royal (1868) on the left - it was later a cinema from 1921. It was on the stage of the Theatre Royal that Sir Henry Irving fell ill; he died that night at the Midland Hotel. The white building opposite is the Regent Cinema, which opened in September 1914. It was called the Essoldo from 1950, and it closed with 'Duel at Rio Bravo' in October 1965. The Yorkshire Penny Bank can be seen at the junction.

SALTAIRE, *The Mill and the Cricket Pitch 1888* 21024

Titus Salt's Victorian idealism led him to believe that a happy, healthy and fulfilled workforce was productive workforce. His model village provided all the essential living amenities, and for recreation he provided a spacious park on the opposite side of the river and canal. Here splendid gardens, with statues of Salt, offered healthy living to the workers at the giant mill. The park was later called Roberts Park, after being bought by another industrialist, and was then offered to Bradford Council.

SALTAIRE
Victoria Road 1909 61869

This area was built by the mill owner Titus Salt as a
model industrial village alongside a canal, river and
railway, well away from the pollution of Bradford.
Provision was made for welfare benefits and help
was given to the aged, infirm and sick. The Club
and Institute, now the Victoria Hall, provided
enlightenment and education for the workers and
their children. Outside the Hall are four sculptured
lions, made for Trafalgar Square, but considered too
small. Only two things were excluded from this
village - a pub and a pawn shop.

SHIPLEY
The Glen 1909 61868

Just on the outskirts of Saltaire lies this beautiful
glen, which in Victorian times was a firm favourite
for a summer-time walk. High above here an
amusement park was established with an aerial ride,
Japanese gardens and a switchback railway.
A toboggan ride also careered down the side of the
glen, but it was closed in 1900 after an accident.
The Glen Tramway is a delightful way to travel to the
top - it has been operating for over a century.

SLAITHWAITE
Seven Arches 1891 28272

Deep in the Colne Valley, Slaithwaite is dominated by the massive Worsted Mills. The main Huddersfield to Manchester railway makes its way along the steep side of the valley, and it has to cross many side valleys. There are two massive bridges in the town, and before the line east reaches another viaduct at Golcar, it passes over these smaller seven arches opposite the town of Linthwaite.

MILNSBRIDGE, *Longwood c1960* M146004

A hundred years ago, Huddersfield was a collection of villages - now Milnsbridge is on the outskirts. The town is packed with mills and machinery works. The tram reached here in 1883, and was the first public system. Trolleybuses took over in 1934. From 1939 the David Brown company manufactured farm tractors in the town. Prime Minister Harold Wilson was born here, and attended New Street Council School.

ELLAND
The Town Hall c1960
E79013

Elland is a small town built around the industries of woollen mills, textiles, and quarries for coal, stone and clay. The railway came to Elland before Halifax: it was on the Manchester to Leeds line from 1839. This Town Hall (1887) was never used for administrative purposes, but rather as a community hall for the town. The clock was added in 1909, and the hall bears the motto of the Savile family: 'Be Fast'.

HORBURY, *Queen Street c1960* H214024

Horbury lies at the heart of the West Yorkshire heavy woollen district. It was the birthplace of the architect John Carr, who started his training in his father's quarry. After a working life based in York, he returned to Horbury to build, at his own expense, the new church of St Peter and St Leonard in 1794. He was later buried here in the vault of the church; the entrance was sealed up in 1884, only to be rediscovered in 1950.

HAREWOOD HOUSE, *c1886* 7365

The West Indies trade in sugar and slaves provided the Lascelles family with their early fortune. The medieval manor house, Gawthorp Hall, was bought by the family, and John Carr was asked to design the new stables block. Shortly afterwards in 1756 he was asked to provide plans for a new house. The foundations of Harewood House were laid in 1759, and work continued for the next 23 years. Gawthorp Hall was demolished, and its foundations now lie beneath the lake. Lancelot 'Capability' Brown landscaped the grounds of this 1800-acre estate, which opened to the public in 1950 and now attracts over 300,000 visitors each year. Hidden within the estate is the exterior of the Emmerdale village where much of the TV series is filmed.

LEEDS, *Duncan Street c1955* L28011

As part of the redevelopment of the central section of Leeds, the Leeds Estates Company embarked on an ambitious scheme to transform the squalor between Vicar Lane and Briggate. With the help of the architect Frank Matcham they created a magnificent series of arcades, which are still much admired. Duncan Street was at the lower end of the development, and never had the most attractive shops. Nevertheless the upper stonework contains some remarkable carvings. The Corn Exchange in the background is one of the finest Victorian structures in the city. Built by Cuthbert Brodrick in 1862, the dome is 75ft high. It was refurbished a decade ago, and provides splendid surroundings for specialist shops.

WETHERBY
The Bridge 1909
61727

The first stone bridge over the Wharfe was constructed in 1233; the bridge we see today was widened in 1826 to cope with the increase in livestock traffic to the town market. The bridge carried the great North Road until Ernest Marples opened a much-needed bypass in 1962. In the year of the photograph a telegraph pole was placed near the bridge; it now carries the town motto, 'Imperium in Imperio' ('a government within another'), an allusion to the county council governing the Rural District.

WETHERBY
The Weir from the Bridge 1909 61736

The weir provided power for the ancient mill that has been here since the time of the Knight's Templars. Behind it was the old brewery, which was used as a billet during the First World War. The brewery chimney came down in 1959, and the remaining building became the site of the bus station. On the outskirts of the town was the Naval Training Ship HMS 'Cabot'. The first arrivals in 1942 were unable to take the rum ration because the security fence was not completed. Lord Haw Haw heard this, and broadcast that HMS 'Cabot' had been sunk - much to the amusement of the locals.

BOSTON SPA, *The Bridge 1908* 59780

This sturdy bridge over the River Wharfe, linking Boston Spa with Thorp Arch, was built in 1770. Along the banks to the east is the old Spa Baths, now converted to housing. A little to the west of here, near the weir, is the old mill, also now luxury houses. Spa water was discovered in 1744 by a farm labourer, John Shires, who was dumb - his mother had cut out his tongue when he was a young boy. Although strenuous efforts were made to place Boston Spa at the forefront of the health resort list, it was always overshadowed by the charms of Harrogate.

BOSTON SPA
Thorp Arch Hall 1895 35186

The lord of the manor, William Gossip, purchased land here with the view to owning a substantial but convenient house in this rural part of the West and North Yorkshire border. He commissioned the designs from the fashionable architect of the time, John Carr of York. Stone came from local quarries within a short distance from here, and even the clay for bricks was found on his land. The house was completed by 1756 - in the same year that William Gossip paid for renovations to the parish church.

BOSTON SPA
Thorp Arch Hall
1908 59782

A closer view of the entrance to the Hall. The designer, John Carr, later went on to be the architect of the magnificent Harewood House. Thorp Arch Hall is now divided into three separate houses, and has been tastefully restored in recent years.

TADCASTER, *The Bridge 1906* 54851

White stone from Tadcaster was used to renovate York Minster; this stone was the reason for the Roman name for this town, Calcaria - meaning 'the white town'. This bridge carried much coaching trade, as it was on the main London to York road. Military action around here included the bloody Battle of Towton in 1461 during the War of the Roses, which resulted in a loss of 28,000 men in one ten-hour battle. The river ran red with blood. The centre of the bridge marks the boundary of the West Riding and the Ainstey of York - a grant of land by King John to the city that contained some twenty villages. Royal visitors were met on the bridge to be escorted to York between 1212 to 1836.

TADCASTER
Grimston Hall 1906 54959

This is the south façade. The old house here was restored and rebuilt in 1840 by Lord Howden to the designs of Decimus Burton, a London architect, who was also responsible for Hyde Park Corner. The stone for Grimston came from the Tadcaster quarries of the Vavasour family from nearby Hazlewood Castle. In 1850 this 800-acre estate was sold to Lord Londesborough, and it was later to be owned by the Fielden family from Todmorden. In the past twenty years the house has been sub-divided into luxury apartments.

YORK, *Bootham Bar 1886* 18443

This was the main exit from the walled city of York. Bootham Bar was built on the site of the Roman gate, and probably much of the stone was re-used. This is one of four major bars in the city; the portcullis and winding gear are still here. In 1832 plans to demolish the whole structure were halted after a public outcry. Steps were added for visitors in 1889. Behind stands the magnificent York Minster.

YORK
Walmgate c1885 18448

This is the principal entrance from the south-east; travellers would then cross the city and leave it at Bootham Bar. Accommodation was added here in the 16th century, and it was lived in until 1960. Walmgate came under heavy attack by cannons and mines in the 1644 siege of York. The Barbican, the security tunnel through the centre arch, was added in the 13th century; it is the only remaining barbican in England.

YORK, *The Cavalry Barracks 1886* 18716

These barracks in Fulford Road were built in 1795 as part of William Pitt's defence programme. They covered 19 acres, including seven for a nursery garden. Around the parade ground there were a bakery, a tailor, a shoemaker, a racket court, a gymnasium and a cricket ground, a hospital and a 20-cell prison. In 1880 the 5th Royal Irish Hussars arrived, and we see them here at sword practice. In 1877 the barracks became part of the much larger Infantry Barracks housing 1350 men. The last horses were retired in 1939, and the Cavalry Barracks were demolished in 1971. The remaining parts became the Imphal Barracks in 1951, named after the West Yorkshire Regiment's defence of the Imphal plains in 1944.

SELBY
The Cross and Finkle Street 1903 49864

The name 'Finkle' comes from a Viking word meaning 'angle' or 'corner', and this less than straight street has not changed its line since those times. There is still a bank on the corner, but the market cross of 1790 is now located to the right of the square, after standing in the park opposite between 1968 and 1986. The railway station opened in the town in 1840, and was the first in the country. The old Toll Bridge, much resented by motorists for the delays caused by cash collection, connected the East and West Ridings, and was bought and made toll free by the council in 1992.

SELBY
The Abbey and the Park 1901 47163

Building started on the abbey in 1100. It was the first to be founded
after the Norman Conquest, and it was not completed until 1935.
Along the way it was abandoned in the dissolution of 1539, the
tower collapsed in 1690 and there was a major fire here in 1906.
This is now a lost view because of the tree growth in the park. Selby
Abbey is now regarded as a world heritage site.

WEST YORKSHIRE

BINGLEY, *The Druid's Altar 1894* 34759

This prominent rock formation stands high up on the St Ives estate over the river; before the age of the car it was holiday treat to walk up here for the exercise and fresh air. The setting was used in Disraeli's novel 'Sybil' - Disraeli stayed here in 1844, when he opened the garden allotments near Cottingley Bridge. So popular was this viewpoint, that its owner temporarily closed it to the public in 1883. For both the VE and VJ days after the war, the altar was the site of celebration beacons.

BINGLEY
Main Street 1926 79085

Bingley was a busy mill town; at one time these numbered nineteen. Here we look in envy at this quiet road - these days it is hard to see the tarmac. Back in the 1920s, people had a good choice of public transport. The tramway from Bradford came here in 1914, but the first road accident happened years earlier in 1900. A 10mph speed limit was imposed in 1903. What council would dare to do that now?

SOUTH YORKSHIRE

BARNSLEY, *The Town Hall c1950* B333008

Built during the dark days of the depression, this was a statement about civic pride. The Town Hall took twenty weeks to complete; it was officially opened on 14 December 1933 by HRH Edward Prince of Wales. It stands high on the hill, looking regally down on the commercial heart of the town.

BARNSLEY
Sheffield Road
c1950 B333001

This was the scene in the central shopping and entertainment centre of Barnsley until the late 1960s; then, in the name of modernisation, the whole area including New Street and Cheapside was demolished to make way for a new market complex. A further redevelopment took place in 1991 with the opening of the Alhambra shopping centre.

BAWTRY, *High Street c1960* B334040

This town on the old Great North Road was specifically created to trade on its location by the local landowner Idonea de Viponts as early as the 12th century, when the existing Roman road was diverted into this huge and attractive market place. Most of the buildings we see here date from the coaching days between 1780 and 1840. The Old House Hotel, left, later became Baines Private Hotel and Tea-rooms. The Town Hall of 1890 (right) became the Working Men's Club and Institute, and the Angel Inn closed in 1907. Cross Wines (near right) was originally the old Hospital of St Mary Magdalene. Bawtry Hall, now a religious centre, was the wartime HQ of No 1 Bomber Command.

BRAMLEY
Main Street c1960
B344006

Bramley lies 2 miles east of Rotherham. There has been little change to this street scene, but now this old manorial town is at a major motorway junction, and is surrounded by huge distribution warehouses.

CONISBOROUGH, *The Castle and the War Memorial c1950* C152003

This Norman stronghold was built on a natural mound as an earth and timber castle in the 12th century. The massive stone keep dates from a century later. Although owned by the Crown from 1461, it was in ruins by 1538. George V and Queen Mary visited the castle on 8 July 1912, only to return the following day to offer condolences to the families of the 35 men lost in the huge explosions at Cadeby Colliery. Coronation Park in the foreground includes the memorial to the soldiers of the Great War, and also the town stocks behind it.

CONISBOROUGH
The Castle Keep 1895 35320

The well-preserved keep stands 90ft high. It is surrounded by
six massive buttresses capable of withstanding cannon and
battering ram attacks.

93

CUDWORTH, *The Village Club and the Cinema c1960* C279005

Cudworth was never a pit village, although it is surrounded by collieries at Monk Bretton (opened in 1870), Carlton (1879), Grimethorpe (1897), Frickley (1905) and Ferrymoor (1917). The Rock Cinema, built on land once owned by the Rock House farm, opened in 1928 showing silent films. It premiered its first talkie on July 1930. It thrived as a village cinema until 1962, when 'Bingola' replaced films. This also faded away a few years ago, and the Rock is now a retail store. The village hall, left, is no longer here, and has been replaced by a nursing home. Dorothy Hyman the Olympic athlete was born in the town, and entered her first hop, skip and jump contest at school in 1953.

DEEPCAR, *From Greenmoor c1950* D97012

Adjacent to Stocksbridge, this town was built on quarrying and the brickworks. Stone from here was used to build Sheffield's Wicker Arches that carried the Manchester railway line from 1848 to 1969. The brickworks chimney was a landmark in the Don Valley from 1891 to 1991.

DONCASTER, *St Sepulchre Gate c1955* D41014

We are looking towards Baxtergate and the Clock Corner (built 1894). We can see the 15th-century tower of St George's church on the horizon (left). This was rebuilt to the designs of Sir Gilbert Scott in 1858 after a major fire five years earlier. On the right are Burton's the tailor and the Nag's Head, built in 1930. The shops and stores on the left were demolished in the last decade to make way for the new Frenchgate shopping centre.

DONCASTER
The Racecourse c1955
D41009

There have been race meetings in Doncaster since 1600, but it was the St Leger of 1776 that put the town on the racing calendar. The race was named after a neighbour of Lord Rockingham, Lt Gen Anthony St Leger. Rockingham commissioned the building of the grandstand in 1778; it was a copy of John Carr's original stand at the York Knavesmire course. A new grandstand opened in 1970.

ECCLESFIELD
The Church 1902 48939

Ecclesfield lies 5 miles north of Sheffield. The village used to be in Derbyshire. Its industry was based on small engineering and the flour mill. The nearby priory was here from as early as 1267. Here we see the church of St Mary the Virgin, which dates from the 12th century (it was renovated in 1866); the font has been in use since 1662. Gas lighting reached the village in 1872, and electricity in the 1930s.

ELSECAR, *Holy Trinity Parish Church c1950* E83008

Elsecar is situated 3 miles south of Barnsley. This is the industrial side of the vast Wentworth Estate: Elsecar was at the forefront of coal exploitation in the 18th century. Initially, the Marquis of Rockingham leased out land for a small mine, but the following year he realised the potential here. He began to exploit this natural resource on his land, in the process becoming one of the biggest producers of coal in South Yorkshire. The old mine was sunk in 1752, with the New Colliery in operation from September 1795. All around were subsidiary trades, such as iron and coal tar. Rockingham also built a short canal to link with the Dearne and Dove Canal. Holy Trinity church was built in 1843, and in 1902 a peal of bells was added as a grateful memorial to the 6th Earl of Fitzwilliam, nephew of Rockingham.

GRENOSIDE
The War Memorial c1950
G119001

This old manorial village 5 miles north of Sheffield was part of the industrial revolution: it established small craft workshops making nails and parts for the burgeoning factories in Sheffield. The land was on the Duke of Norfolk's estate - at one time he was the country's richest man. His name lives on in the village: Norfolk Hill goes up to the right, and opposite on Sheffield Road is the Norfolk Arms Hotel.

NEW ROSSINGTON, *Queen Mary's Road c1950* N73003

The small village based around the manor of Rossington was enlarged to its west side once coal reserves had been found. The first pit was sunk in September 1912, and a 'New' Rossington was created for the colliers and their families. This small town was built in a radial pattern, and soon contained all the ingredients of urban life - the Co-op opened in 1915, the Royal Hotel (right) in 1921, and the Methodist church beyond it in 1928. A bus service came in 1922, and at the end of the road on the right, the Hippodrome Cinema entertained the town from 1929 until June 1962.

OUGHTIBRIDGE
The View over the Valley c1960 O50014

As nearby Sheffield expanded, so did towns like Oughtibridge in the Don Valley. The river powered mills, but later manufacturing became the mainstay. Here high up over the town, in 1951 the Wortley Rural District Council thoughtfully placed this beacon to mark the Festival of Britain. It shows a map of the area with distance and altitude. Sheffield at 275ft is four miles away, while the South Yorkshire Mental Hospital (375ft) is a mile from here.

PENISTONE, *The Railway Bridge c1960* P154006

This 29-arch viaduct carries the Sheffield to Huddersfield railway over the River Don. It was built in 1849 a short distance from Penistone station. In 1916, disaster struck: the second and third arches collapsed, causing a tank engine to crash down into the debris. At an elevation of 747ft, Penistone always suffers with the weather, particularly in the ferocious winters of 1933, 1947 and 1963.

ROTHERHAM
The Parish Church c1950 R60018

A church has been on this central site from AD 937. All Saints' parish
church was restored in 1873 by Sir Gilbert Scott (he was also
responsible for Doncaster's St George's church). The 180ft-high spire
dominates the town, and looks down onto the heart of the shopping
area. The churchyard contained 1800 graves; it was closed in 1854,
with many of the stones being removed in 1932 and 1950 during the
creation of All Saints' Square.

ROTHERHAM
The Hospital 1895
36242

As the town became
more industrialised,
the old Dispensary (in
College Street since
1828) was replaced by
this fine hospital in
1872, built in Babb's
Croft along the
Doncaster Road.

ROYSTON, *The Wells, Station Road c1950* R248005

This small village, 3 miles north of Barnsley, is in the heart of the coal mining country. This view is hardly changed, except
for a new retail development out of the picture on the left. On the Bethel Church of 1803 (centre) is this positive message:
'Come sinners for the gospel fear. Ye need not be left behind, for God has bidden all mankind'.

BEAUCHIEF
c1950 B335012

Beauchief is now a northern suburb of Sheffield, but it was once part of Derbyshire. The abbey was built here during Norman times, and after the Dissolution the area was given to local landowners. Much of the stone from the abbey tower was used to build the local church a century later. Beauchief Hall was also constructed from the remaining stone.

SHEFFIELD, *Fargate 1893* 31961

We are at the heart of the city centre, and this is now all pedestrianised. The Albany Hotel, dating from the late 1870s, was originally a Temperance establishment. The YMCA building to the left of the complex was added in 1891. The frontage of the hotel has changed with the removal of the top windows and decoration. The obelisk commemorated Queen Victoria's Jubilee in 1887. It was removed to Endcliffe Woods in 1903; a statue of the Queen replaced it here in 1905, but it was itself taken to the woods in 1930.

SPROTBOROUGH, *The Bridge 1895* 35326

This fine seven-arch Grecian-style bridge over the River Don was built in 1850; it linked the village to Warmsworth, and replaced the ferry service. From the late 17th century, Sprotborough Hall dominated the village for three hundred years, before death duties forced its sale in September 1925. It was demolished six months later, and new houses were built in the park. Sir Walter Scott stayed in the village whilst writing his novel 'Ivanhoe'.

STOCKSBRIDGE
The Clock Tower c1950
S324016

The industrialisation of the Don Valley begins here at Stocksbridge, a town dominated by steel, chemicals and former coal and clay workings. Samuel Fox's umbrella works were here, as well as the English Fruit Preserving Co's orchards. Here at the top of Nanny Hill on the way to the cemetery stands the Clock Tower, built between 1920 and 1923 as a war memorial.

THORNE
Market Place c1955
T303029

Ascend the clock tower of St Nicholas's parish church and see six of the county's major rivers - the Humber, the Don, the Went, the Ouse, the Trent and the Aire. Flood defences were needed here, which were devised by the Dutch engineer, Cornelius Vermuyden. In the late 19th century, many workers from Holland were attracted to this land of canals and windmills as skilled peat workers. The White Hart, left, was an old coaching inn, restored in 1737, and the bank on the right used to be Lester's barber's shop. Thomas Crapper, inventor of the flushing toilet, was born in Thorne in 1837.

TICKHILL
Market Place c1955
T136022

In medieval times Tickhill, which lies 4 miles south of Doncaster, was more important than Sheffield; its castle, built about 1130, was one of the most important in the north - we can just see the castle mound (centre horizon). The Buttercross (centre left), erected in 1777, was restored in 1898. Behind it is the post office and library. The town has escaped industry, and because of this the South Yorkshire Joint Railway did not arrive until 1908.

COASTAL YORKSHIRE

STAITHES, *The Harbour c1885* 18215

This intriguing historical fishing village lies between two prominent headlands, Penny Nab and Cowbar Nab. Walk around Staithes, and the past is along every alleyway. Red-tiled cottages are squeezed into narrow passages that rise dramatically from seashore to cliff top. A young James Cook started his working life here as an apprentice grocer, before the lure of the sea took him around the world on his voyages of discovery.

RUNSWICK
The Village c1885
18204

Two hundred years before this photograph, the old Runswick collapsed into the sea during a violent storm. Undaunted, the villagers rebuilt their cottages further up the cliff. Their view of the turbulent and cruel North Sea is a potent reminder of this vulnerable location.

RUNSWICK, *The Village 1927* 80193

Victorian visitors soon discovered this rugged village once the railway opened up the dramatic Yorkshire coast in 1883. City dwellers from West Yorkshire flooded in to take in the sights of this picture postcard village. Artists and painters also appreciated the vistas and light in this village, perched on the edge of the cliffs.

SANDSEND
General View 1901 46807

This is a village of two halves, each bisected by fast-running streams rushing towards the sea. Sandsend was once a centre for alum mining, and remains can still be observed along the coast. Two castles, one in ruins, the other inhabited, can be discovered just inland, high in the Mulgrave woods. The railway viaduct dominated the village from 1883 until its demolition in 1958.
Fortunately, the station was saved; it is now a private residence with stunning sea views.

SALTWICK BAY
The Nab 1913 66297A

This dramatic rock formation lies just south of Whitby, on the Cleveland way, along the old railway track. High above the bay on the cliffs is the Whitby lighthouse; its powerful fog horn is capable of blasting a warning signal ten miles out to sea.

ROBIN HOOD'S BAY
General View 1927 80184

Robin Hood's Bay is now half the size of the original village – the centre section slid into the sea, taking with it the new road. What remains is a fascinating jigsaw of cobbled alleyways and compact fishing cottages. Gardens have been reused for new cottages, and extra storeys have been added for deserving relatives. The old railway journey around the bay must have been a breathtaking experience. Life in the village was chronicled by Leo Walmsley in his novel 'Three Fevers'. In 1935 it was made into a classic film, 'Turn of the Tide'.

RAVENSCAR, *The Terrace and Robin Hood's Bay 1901* 46804

High on the 600ft cliff and looking towards Robin Hood's Bay is the Raven Hall Hotel, once the site of a Roman signal station. In 1900 plans were unveiled to create a new holiday resort at Ravenscar. Sad to say, investors were unimpressed, and only the road layout and a hotel block and shops were built. In 1912 the charms of the coast were captured in films made by the Robin Hood Film Co from Bradford. The actors stayed at Peak Farm and Corby House during their twelve weeks of summer shooting on location. All the film stock was stored in the stables at the hotel. Unfortunately, they were destroyed in a fire before the films, 'The Dangerous Edge' and 'Smugglers Cave', could be publicly shown, although before the disaster the actors did see a preview at the Londesborough Cinema in Scarborough.

HACKNESS
The Park and Lake
c1877 9550

Just inland from Scarborough, along the Forge Valley, lies the peaceful village of Hackness. The imposing 18th-century Hackness Hall was built here on the site of an old priory to the designs of John Carr's assistant Thomas Atkinson. The gardens and lake were laid out later. The house survived, and has recently been converted to a luxury hotel.

SCARBOROUGH
South Bay 1897
39333

Here we see the Queen of the Resorts in all its glory. On the right the bay is dominated by the Grand Hotel (1867), designed by Cuthbert Brodrick from Leeds, and in the centre is Sir Joseph Paxton's splendid Spa Hall and Theatre (1880). The cliff railway, the first in the country, opened in 1875.

SCARBOROUGH
The Beach c1885 18237

Punch and Judy hold the attention of the formally-dressed crowd of holidaymakers in the South Bay. At low tide, these broad sands offer plenty of space for youngsters to enjoy their summer fun. The bathing machines at the water's edge kept Victorian eyes away from the modesty of those who braved the brine. On the horizon the remains of the Norman castle stand on land once in use as a Roman signalling point. Thomas Warwick's Revolving Viewing Tower, set high on the cliffs near the castle, was a short-lived Victorian attraction from 1897 to 1907 - it was demolished after being described an eyesore by South Bay residents.

WHITBY
Tin Ghaut 1913 66292

This was one of the many narrow alleyways leading down to the harbour area. From here children could play safely, and the fishermen could prepare their nets and their boats. Tin Ghaut was just off Grape Lane, once home to Whitby explorer Captain James Cook, who is remembered in monuments and museums all around the north-east coast. This charming view no longer exists. Tin Ghaut was demolished in 1959 to make way for a car park.

WHITBY
The Harbour 1885 18168

In the year of this photograph, Whitby is poised for a summer influx of new visitors via the new Scarborough to Whitby Railway, which opened on 6 July 1885. Down in the harbour, the tall ship is moored just in front of the Angel Vaults, still here as a waterside inn. The parish church and the abbey ruins on the horizon are reached by the 199 steps from the old part of town. In AD644 the date of Easter was fixed here in a meeting between the Celtic and Roman churches - the meeting was known as the Synod of Whitby. In between the tall houses on the far right of the harbour was Tin Ghaut - see 66292.

WHITBY, *The Quay 1927* 80177

Visitors come here even today to look at the catches brought in by Whitby trawlers. A new fish market exists on this site, but little else is changed; the lighthouse on the new pier still guides ships back into the shelter of this welcoming harbour.

FILEY
Church Ravine 1890
23482

St Oswald's church at the top of this ravine used to be on the edge of the East Riding. Older folk referred to eventually 'visiting the North Riding' - the site of the church's graveyard. Stretching down from the north side of town towards the coble landing, Filey is still a mixture of a fishing village and a Victorian resort. From the coble landing there is a splendid walk out to sea on the mile-long rock promontory, the Brigg. Billy Butlin placed Filey firmly on the summer map when he opened his third holiday camp here in 1939. Although it was requisitioned by the RAF during the war, it re-opened in 1946 to a tired nation in desperate need of fun and relaxation. Changes in holiday expectations caused its closure in 1993. A short-lived plan to reopen the camp three years later ended in bankruptcy.

INDEX

Addingham 72

Adel 73

Askrigg 31, 32-33, 34

Aysgarth 37

Bainbridge 30-31

Barnsley 90, 91

Bawtry 91

Beauchief 101

Bellerby 40, 41

Bingley 87, 88-89

Boroughbridge 54-55, 56

Boston Spa 81, 82

Bradford 74, 75

Bramley 92

Carperby 34-35

Conisborough 92, 93

Coverham 47

Crakehall 50-51

Cudworth 94

Deepcar 94

Doncaster 95

Downholme 19

Easby 58

East Witton 48

Ecclesfield 96

Egton 59

Elland 78

Elsecar 96

Filey 112-113

Gilling West 21

Grassington 71

Grenoside 97

Grinton 18

Gunnerside 15

Hackness 108

Harewood House 79

Harrogate 61, 62-63, 64

Hauxwell 43, 44-45

Hawes 29

Horbury 78

Hubberholme 70

Hudswell Bank 20

Ilkley 72

Ingleton 66

Jervaulx Abbey 47

Keld 13, 14

Kettlewell 69

Knaresborough 64, 65

Langcliffe 68

Leeds 79

Leyburn 42-43

Malham Cove 69

Marrick 18

Masham 50

Middleham 46

Milnsbridge 77

Nappa 34

New Rossington 97

Oughtibridge 98

Pateley Bridge 12, 60

Penistone 98

Preston-under-Scar 37

Ravenscar 108

Ravensworth 20-21

Redmire 36-37

Reeth 15

Richmond 22-23, 24-25, 26, 27

Rievaulx Abbey 57

Ripon 52, 53

Robin Hood's Bay 107

Rotherham 99, 100

Royston 100

Runswick 105

Saltaire 75, 76

Saltwick Bay 106

Sandsend 106

Scarborough 108-109

Scorton 27

Scruton 50

Selby 85, 86

Settle 67

Sheffield 101

Shipley 76

Skeeby 28

Skelton on Ure 53

Slaithwaite 77

Sleights 59

Snape 49

Spennithorne 48

Sprotborough 102

Staithes 104

Stalling Busk 31

Starbotton 71

Stocksbridge 102

Studley Royal 51, 52

Swaledale 16-17

Tadcaster 82, 83

Thorne 102-103

Thornton Dale 58

Tickhill 103

Wensley 41, 42

West Burton 10, 38

West Witton 38-39, 40

Wetherby 80-81

Whitby 110, 111

York 83, 84

Frith Book Co Titles

www.francisfrith.co.uk

The Frith Book Company publishes over 100 new titles each year. A selection of those currently available are listed below. For latest catalogue please contact Frith Book Co.

Town Books 96 pages, approximately 100 photos. **County and Themed Books** 128 pages, approximately 150 photos (unless specified). All titles hardback with laminated case and jacket, except those indicated pb (paperback)

Title	ISBN	Price	Title	ISBN	Price
Amersham, Chesham & Rickmansworth (pb)	1-85937-340-2	£9.99	Devon (pb)	1-85937-297-x	£9.99
Andover (pb)	1-85937-292-9	£9.99	Devon Churches (pb)	1-85937-250-3	£9.99
Aylesbury (pb)	1-85937-227-9	£9.99	Dorchester (pb)	1-85937-307-0	£9.99
Barnstaple (pb)	1-85937-300-3	£9.99	Dorset (pb)	1-85937-269-4	£9.99
Basildon Living Memories (pb)	1-85937-515-4	£9.99	Dorset Coast (pb)	1-85937-299-6	£9.99
Bath (pb)	1-85937-419-0	£9.99	Dorset Living Memories (pb)	1-85937-584-7	£9.99
Bedford (pb)	1-85937-205-8	£9.99	Down the Severn (pb)	1-85937-560-x	£9.99
Bedfordshire Living Memories	1-85937-513-8	£14.99	Down The Thames (pb)	1-85937-278-3	£9.99
Belfast (pb)	1-85937-303-8	£9.99	Down the Trent	1-85937-311-9	£14.99
Berkshire (pb)	1-85937-191-4	£9.99	East Anglia (pb)	1-85937-265-1	£9.99
Berkshire Churches	1-85937-170-1	£17.99	East Grinstead (pb)	1-85937-138-8	£9.99
Berkshire Living Memories	1-85937-332-1	£14.99	East London	1-85937-080-2	£14.99
Black Country	1-85937-497-2	£12.99	East Sussex (pb)	1-85937-606-1	£9.99
Blackpool (pb)	1-85937-393-3	£9.99	Eastbourne (pb)	1-85937-399-2	£9.99
Bognor Regis (pb)	1-85937-431-x	£9.99	Edinburgh (pb)	1-85937-193-0	£8.99
Bournemouth (pb)	1-85937-545-6	£9.99	England In The 1880s	1-85937-331-3	£17.99
Bradford (pb)	1-85937-204-x	£9.99	Essex - Second Selection	1-85937-456-5	£14.99
Bridgend (pb)	1-85937-386-0	£7.99	Essex (pb)	1-85937-270-8	£9.99
Bridgwater (pb)	1-85937-305-4	£9.99	Essex Coast	1-85937-342-9	£14.99
Bridport (pb)	1-85937-327-5	£9.99	Essex Living Memories	1-85937-490-5	£14.99
Brighton (pb)	1-85937-192-2	£8.99	Exeter	1-85937-539-1	£9.99
Bristol (pb)	1-85937-264-3	£9.99	Exmoor (pb)	1-85937-608-8	£9.99
British Life A Century Ago (pb)	1-85937-213-9	£9.99	Falmouth (pb)	1-85937-594-4	£9.99
Buckinghamshire (pb)	1-85937-200-7	£9.99	Folkestone (pb)	1-85937-124-8	£9.99
Camberley (pb)	1-85937-222-8	£9.99	Frome (pb)	1-85937-317-8	£9.99
Cambridge (pb)	1-85937-422-0	£9.99	Glamorgan	1-85937-488-3	£14.99
Cambridgeshire (pb)	1-85937-420-4	£9.99	Glasgow (pb)	1-85937-190-6	£9.99
Cambridgeshire Villages	1-85937-523-5	£14.99	Glastonbury (pb)	1-85937-338-0	£7.99
Canals And Waterways (pb)	1-85937-291-0	£9.99	Gloucester (pb)	1-85937-232-5	£9.99
Canterbury Cathedral (pb)	1-85937-179-5	£9.99	Gloucestershire (pb)	1-85937-561-8	£9.99
Cardiff (pb)	1-85937-093-4	£9.99	Great Yarmouth (pb)	1-85937-426-3	£9.99
Carmarthenshire (pb)	1-85937-604-5	£9.99	Greater Manchester (pb)	1-85937-266-x	£9.99
Chelmsford (pb)	1-85937-310-0	£9.99	Guildford (pb)	1-85937-410-7	£9.99
Cheltenham (pb)	1-85937-095-0	£9.99	Hampshire (pb)	1-85937-279-1	£9.99
Cheshire (pb)	1-85937-271-6	£9.99	Harrogate (pb)	1-85937-423-9	£9.99
Chester (pb)	1-85937-382 8	£9.99	Hastings and Bexhill (pb)	1-85937-131-0	£9.99
Chesterfield (pb)	1-85937-378-x	£9.99	Heart of Lancashire (pb)	1-85937-197-3	£9.99
Chichester (pb)	1-85937-228-7	£9.99	Helston (pb)	1-85937-214-7	£9.99
Churches of East Cornwall (pb)	1-85937-249-x	£9.99	Hereford (pb)	1-85937-175-2	£9.99
Churches of Hampshire (pb)	1-85937-207-4	£9.99	Herefordshire (pb)	1-85937-567-7	£9.99
Cinque Ports & Two Ancient Towns	1-85937-492-1	£14.99	Herefordshire Living Memories	1-85937-514-6	£14.99
Colchester (pb)	1-85937-188-4	£8.99	Hertfordshire (pb)	1-85937-247-3	£9.99
Cornwall (pb)	1-85937-229-5	£9.99	Horsham (pb)	1-85937-432-8	£9.99
Cornwall Living Memories	1-85937-248-1	£14.99	Humberside (pb)	1-85937-605-3	£9.99
Cotswolds (pb)	1-85937-230-9	£9.99	Hythe, Romney Marsh, Ashford (pb)	1-85937-256-2	£9.99
Cotswolds Living Memories	1-85937-255-4	£14.99	Ipswich (pb)	1-85937-424-7	£9.99
County Durham (pb)	1-85937-398-4	£9.99	Isle of Man (pb)	1-85937-268-6	£9.99
Croydon Living Memories (pb)	1-85937-162-0	£9.99	Isle of Wight (pb)	1-85937-429-8	£9.99
Cumbria (pb)	1-85937-621-5	£9.99	Isle of Wight Living Memories	1-85937-304-6	£14.99
Derby (pb)	1-85937-367-4	£9.99	Kent (pb)	1-85937-189-2	£9.99
Derbyshire (pb)	1-85937-196-5	£9.99	Kent Living Memories(pb)	1-85937-401-8	£9.99
Derbyshire Living Memories	1-85937-330-5	£14.99	Kings Lynn (pb)	1-85937-334-8	£9.99

Available from your local bookshop or from the publisher

Frith Book Co Titles (continued)

Title	ISBN	Price	Title	ISBN	Price
Lake District (pb)	1-85937-275-9	£9.99	Sherborne (pb)	1-85937-301-1	£9.99
Lancashire Living Memories	1-85937-335-6	£14.99	Shrewsbury (pb)	1-85937-325-9	£9.99
Lancaster, Morecambe, Heysham (pb)	1-85937-233-3	£9.99	Shropshire (pb)	1-85937-326-7	£9.99
Leeds (pb)	1-85937-202-3	£9.99	Shropshire Living Memories	1-85937-643-6	£14.99
Leicester (pb)	1-85937-381-x	£9.99	Somerset	1-85937-153-1	£14.99
Leicestershire & Rutland Living Memories	1-85937-500-6	£12.99	South Devon Coast	1-85937-107-8	£14.99
Leicestershire (pb)	1-85937-185-x	£9.99	South Devon Living Memories (pb)	1-85937-609-6	£9.99
Lighthouses	1-85937-257-0	£9.99	South East London (pb)	1-85937-263-5	£9.99
Lincoln (pb)	1-85937-380-1	£9.99	South Somerset	1-85937-318-6	£14.99
Lincolnshire (pb)	1-85937-433-6	£9.99	South Wales	1-85937-519-7	£14.99
Liverpool and Merseyside (pb)	1-85937-234-1	£9.99	Southampton (pb)	1-85937-427-1	£9.99
London (pb)	1-85937-183-3	£9.99	Southend (pb)	1-85937-313-5	£9.99
London Living Memories	1-85937-454-9	£14.99	Southport (pb)	1-85937-425-5	£9.99
Ludlow (pb)	1-85937-176-0	£9.99	St Albans (pb)	1-85937-341-0	£9.99
Luton (pb)	1-85937-235-x	£9.99	St Ives (pb)	1-85937-415-8	£9.99
Maidenhead (pb)	1-85937-339-9	£9.99	Stafford Living Memories (pb)	1-85937-503-0	£9.99
Maidstone (pb)	1-85937-391-7	£9.99	Staffordshire (pb)	1-85937-308-9	£9.99
Manchester (pb)	1-85937-198-1	£9.99	Stourbridge (pb)	1-85937-530-8	£9.99
Marlborough (pb)	1-85937-336-4	£9.99	Stratford upon Avon (pb)	1-85937-388-7	£9.99
Middlesex	1-85937-158-2	£14.99	Suffolk (pb)	1-85937-221-x	£9.99
Monmouthshire	1-85937-532-4	£14.99	Suffolk Coast (pb)	1-85937-610-x	£9.99
New Forest (pb)	1-85937-390-9	£9.99	Surrey (pb)	1-85937-240-6	£9.99
Newark (pb)	1-85937-366-6	£9.99	Surrey Living Memories	1-85937-328-3	£14.99
Newport, Wales (pb)	1-85937-258-9	£9.99	Sussex (pb)	1-85937-184-1	£9.99
Newquay (pb)	1-85937-421-2	£9.99	Sutton (pb)	1-85937-337-2	£9.99
Norfolk (pb)	1-85937-195-7	£9.99	Swansea (pb)	1-85937-167-1	£9.99
Norfolk Broads	1-85937-486-7	£14.99	Taunton (pb)	1-85937-314-3	£9.99
Norfolk Living Memories (pb)	1-85937-402-6	£9.99	Tees Valley & Cleveland (pb)	1-85937-623-1	£9.99
North Buckinghamshire	1-85937-626-6	£14.99	Teignmouth (pb)	1-85937-370-4	£7.99
North Devon Living Memories	1-85937-261-9	£14.99	Thanet (pb)	1-85937-116-7	£9.99
North Hertfordshire	1-85937-547-2	£14.99	Tiverton (pb)	1-85937-178-7	£9.99
North London (pb)	1-85937-403-4	£9.99	Torbay (pb)	1-85937-597-9	£9.99
North Somerset	1-85937-302-x	£14.99	Truro (pb)	1-85937-598-7	£9.99
North Wales (pb)	1-85937-298-8	£9.99	Victorian & Edwardian Dorset	1-85937-254-6	£14.99
North Yorkshire (pb)	1-85937-236-8	£9.99	Victorian & Edwardian Kent (pb)	1-85937-624-X	£9.99
Northamptonshire Living Memories	1-85937-529-4	£14.99	Victorian & Edwardian Maritime Album (pb)	1-85937-622-3	£9.99
Northamptonshire	1-85937-150-7	£14.99	Victorian and Edwardian Sussex (pb)	1-85937-625-8	£9.99
Northumberland Tyne & Wear (pb)	1-85937-281-3	£9.99	Villages of Devon (pb)	1-85937-293-7	£9.99
Northumberland	1-85937-522-7	£14.99	Villages of Kent (pb)	1-85937-294-5	£9.99
Norwich (pb)	1-85937-194-9	£8.99	Villages of Sussex (pb)	1-85937-295-3	£9.99
Nottingham (pb)	1-85937-324-0	£9.99	Warrington (pb)	1-85937-507-3	£9.99
Nottinghamshire (pb)	1-85937-187-6	£9.99	Warwick (pb)	1-85937-518-9	£9.99
Oxford (pb)	1-85937-411-5	£9.99	Warwickshire (pb)	1-85937-203-1	£9.99
Oxfordshire (pb)	1-85937-430-1	£9.99	Welsh Castles (pb)	1-85937-322-4	£9.99
Oxfordshire Living Memories	1-85937-525-1	£14.99	West Midlands (pb)	1-85937-289-9	£9.99
Paignton (pb)	1-85937-374-7	£7.99	West Sussex (pb)	1-85937-607-x	£9.99
Peak District (pb)	1-85937-280-5	£9.99	West Yorkshire (pb)	1-85937-201-5	£9.99
Pembrokeshire	1-85937-262-7	£14.99	Weston Super Mare (pb)	1-85937-306-2	£9.99
Penzance (pb)	1-85937-595-2	£9.99	Weymouth (pb)	1-85937-209-0	£9.99
Peterborough (pb)	1-85937-219-8	£9.99	Wiltshire (pb)	1-85937-277-5	£9.99
Picturesque Harbours	1-85937-208-2	£14.99	Wiltshire Churches (pb)	1-85937-171-x	£9.99
Piers	1-85937-237-6	£17.99	Wiltshire Living Memories (pb)	1-85937-396-8	£9.99
Plymouth (pb)	1-85937-389-5	£9.99	Winchester (pb)	1-85937-428-x	£9.99
Poole & Sandbanks (pb)	1-85937-251-1	£9.99	Windsor (pb)	1-85937-333-x	£9.99
Preston (pb)	1-85937-212-0	£9.99	Wokingham & Bracknell (pb)	1-85937-329-1	£9.99
Reading (pb)	1-85937-238-4	£9.99	Woodbridge (pb)	1-85937-498-0	£9.99
Redhill to Reigate (pb)	1-85937-596-0	£9.99	Worcester (pb)	1-85937-165-5	£9.99
Ringwood (pb)	1-85937-384-4	£7.99	Worcestershire Living Memories	1-85937-489-1	£14.99
Romford (pb)	1-85937-319-4	£9.99	Worcestershire	1-85937-152-3	£14.99
Royal Tunbridge Wells (pb)	1-85937-504-9	£9.99	York (pb)	1-85937-199-x	£9.99
Salisbury (pb)	1-85937-239-2	£9.99	Yorkshire (pb)	1-85937-186-8	£9.99
Scarborough (pb)	1-85937-379-8	£9.99	Yorkshire Coastal Memories	1-85937-506-5	£14.99
Sevenoaks and Tonbridge (pb)	1-85937-392-5	£9.99	Yorkshire Dales	1-85937-502-2	£14.99
Sheffield & South Yorks (pb)	1-85937-267-8	£9.99	Yorkshire Living Memories (pb)	1-85937-397-6	£9.99

See Frith books on the internet at www.francisfrith.co.uk

FRITH PRODUCTS & SERVICES

Francis Frith would doubtless be pleased to know that the pioneering publishing venture he started in 1860 still continues today. Over a hundred and forty years later, The Francis Frith Collection continues in the same innovative tradition and is now one of the foremost publishers of vintage photographs in the world. Some of the current activities include:

Interior Decoration

Today Frith's photographs can be seen framed and as giant wall murals in thousands of pubs, restaurants, hotels, banks, retail stores and other public buildings throughout the country. In every case they enhance the unique local atmosphere of the places they depict and provide reminders of gentler days in an increasingly busy and frenetic world.

Product Promotions

Frith products are used by many major companies to promote the sales of their own products or to reinforce their own history and heritage. Frith promotions have been used by Hovis bread, Courage beers, Scots Porage Oats, Colman's mustard, Cadbury's foods, Mellow Birds coffee, Dunhill pipe tobacco, Guinness, and Bulmer's Cider.

Genealogy and Family History

As the interest in family history and roots grows world-wide, more and more people are turning to Frith's photographs of Great Britain for images of the towns, villages and streets where their ancestors lived; and, of course, photographs of the churches and chapels where their ancestors were christened, married and buried are an essential part of every genealogy tree and family album.

Frith Products

All Frith photographs are available Framed or just as Mounted Prints and Posters (size 23 x 16 inches). These may be ordered from the address below. From time to time other products - Address Books, Calendars, Table Mats, etc - are available.

The Internet

Already fifty thousand Frith photographs can be viewed and purchased on the internet through the Frith websites and a myriad of partner sites.

For more detailed information on Frith companies and products, look at these sites:

www.francisfrith.co.uk
www.francisfrith.com
(for North American visitors)

See the complete list of Frith Books at:

www.francisfrith.co.uk

This web site is regularly updated with the latest list of publications from the Frith Book Company. If you wish to buy books relating to another part of the country that your local bookshop does not stock, you may purchase on-line.

For further information, trade, or author enquiries please contact us at the address below:
The Francis Frith Collection, Frith's Barn, Teffont, Salisbury, Wiltshire, England SP3 5QP.
Tel: +44 (0)1722 716 376 Fax: +44 (0)1722 716 881 Email: sales@francisfrith.co.uk

See Frith books on the internet at www.francisfrith.co.uk

FREE PRINT OF YOUR CHOICE

Mounted Print
Overall size 14 x 11 inches (355 x 280mm)

Choose any Frith photograph in this book.
Simply complete the Voucher opposite and return it with your remittance for £2.25 (to cover postage and handling) and we will print the photograph of your choice in SEPIA (size 11 x 8 inches) and supply it in a cream mount with a burgundy rule line (overall size 14 x 11 inches).
Please note: photographs with a reference number starting with a "Z" are not Frith photographs and cannot be supplied under this offer.
Offer valid for delivery to UK addresses only.

PLUS: Order additional Mounted Prints at HALF PRICE - £7.49 each (normally £14.99)
If you would like to order more Frith prints from this book, possibly as gifts for friends and family, you can buy them at half price (with no additional postage and handling costs).

PLUS: Have your Mounted Prints framed
For an extra £14.95 per print you can have your mounted print(s) framed in an elegant polished wood and gilt moulding, overall size 16 x 13 inches (no additional postage and handling required).

IMPORTANT!

These special prices are only available if you use this form to order . You must use the ORIGINAL VOUCHER on this page (no copies permitted). We can only despatch to one address. This offer cannot be combined with any other offer.

Send completed Voucher form to:
The Francis Frith Collection, Frith's Barn, Teffont, Salisbury, Wiltshire SP3 5QP

CHOOSE A PHOTOGRAPH FROM THIS BOOK

Voucher for **FREE** and Reduced Price Frith Prints

Please do not photocopy this voucher. Only the original is valid, so please fill it in, cut it out and return it to us with your order.

Picture ref no	Page no	Qty	Mounted @ £7.49	Framed + £14.95	Total Cost
		1	Free of charge*	£	£
			£7.49	£	£
			£7.49	£	£
			£7.49	£	£
			£7.49	£	£
			£7.49	£	£
Please allow 28 days for delivery			* Post & handling (UK)		£2.25
			Total Order Cost		£

Title of this book . . . .

I enclose a cheque/postal order for £ . . . .
made payable to 'The Francis Frith Collection'

OR please debit my Mastercard / Visa / Switch (Maestro) /Amex card
(credit cards please on all overseas orders), details below

Card Number

Issue No (Switch only)   Valid from (Amex/Switch)

Expires   Signature

Name Mr/Mrs/Ms . . . .
Address . . . .
. . . .
. . . .
. . . . Postcode . . . .
Daytime Tel No . . . .
Email . . . .

Valid to 31/12/07

Would you like to find out more about Francis Frith?

We have recently recruited some entertaining speakers who are happy to visit local groups, clubs and societies to give an illustrated talk documenting Frith's travels and photographs. If you are a member of such a group and are interested in hosting a presentation, we would love to hear from you.

Our speakers bring with them a small selection of our local town and county books, together with sample prints. They are happy to take orders. A small proportion of the order value is donated to the group who have hosted the presentation. The talks are therefore an excellent way of fundraising for small groups and societies.

Can you help us with information about any of the Frith photographs in this book?

We are gradually compiling an historical record for each of the photographs in the Frith archive. It is always fascinating to find out the names of the people shown in the pictures, as well as insights into the shops, buildings and other features depicted.

If you recognize anyone in the photographs in this book, or if you have information not already included in the author's caption, do let us know. We would love to hear from you, and will try to publish it in future books or articles.

Our production team

Frith books are produced by a small dedicated team at offices in the converted Grade II listed 18th-century barn at Teffont near Salisbury, illustrated above. Most have worked with the Frith Collection for many years. All have in common one quality: they have a passion for the Frith Collection. The team is constantly expanding, but currently includes:

Paul Baron, Phillip Brennan, Jason Buck, John Buck, Ruth Butler, Heather Crisp, David Davies, Louis du Mont, Isobel Hall, Gareth Harris, Lucy Hart, Julian Hight, Peter Horne, James Kinnear, Karen Kinnear, Tina Leary, Stuart Login, David Marsh, Lesley-Ann Millard, Sue Molloy, Glenda Morgan, Wayne Morgan, Sarah Roberts, Kate Rotondetto, Dean Scource, Eliza Sackett, Terence Sackett, Sandra Sampson, Adrian Sanders, Sandra Sanger, Jan Scrivens, Julia Skinner, David Smith, Miles Smith, Lewis Taylor, Shelley Tolcher, Lorraine Tuck, Amanita Wainwright and Ricky Williams.

Free Print – see overleaf